Beer, Aidsbabies & Enlightenment

Contents

Important: Have you already been through a process of serious self-enquiry? Are you a spiritual or non-dual teacher? Then please feel free to go straight to chapter 15.

1. Novitius

'Novitius!'

'Oh shit shit shit,' I mumble. 'Erm... yes sir.'

'Novitius! What are you doing there? Goddammit, are you pressing or something?'

'Pressing,' I answer, 'what does that mean?'

'Pressing means doing nothing, Novitius, and we really don't like that at the USF.'

'Novitius is pressing here really really hard!' yells a large, round fourth-year member of the fraternity.

Immediately three of his sweaty, drunken, equally fat friends come running towards me.

'Novitius is pressing like crazy! On your knees Novitius... *now!*'

Silently I get to my knees.

'If we see you pressing once more, then you're out of here—home! *Understood?*'

'Yes, sir.'

'Now fuck off, you filthy piece of shit!'

'Chill atmosphere,' I think.

We are thirty kilometres outside the city of Utrecht,

somewhere in a hilly nature reserve in the province of Utrecht in the Netherlands. In all there are a hundred and eighty of us Novitii, students who are undergoing the initiation week at the USF, the Utrecht Student Fraternity. We are ripping pine saplings out of the ground with our bare hands. In short, horrible heavy work.

The two weeks of the initiation consist of a systematic programme of humiliation, hard work and little sleep. The first day starts with us being chased like wild cattle, after which we have to stuff our meals into our mouths in five minutes flat, whilst simultaneously being drilled in the rules of the fraternity.

Running pointlessly around, doing meaningless jobs, being insulted... forced to kneel down then to stand up, standing in lines for hours on end... spending an afternoon crawling around in rotten fish—these are just the highlights of the first week.

In the second week we have to sing for hours on end whilst drunken fraternity members throw beer in our faces, after which we have to do pointless jobs in town and endure all sorts of other inconveniences.

It culminates in one final evening where all of us Novitii are completely shaken to bits by hundreds of drunken older members. For me, it's the final straw.

I walk up to the boss of the USF who, for a change, is standing apart from the main group of tormentors.

'Novitius!' he yells at me as he sees me approach.

'Yes, sir. Or I can call you Nils now?'

'What! You dare to call me Nils?! You've got some nerve, Novitius!'

'Indeed I have, Nils.'

'What do you want, Novitius? Don't you realise that in ten minutes the initiation will be over and done with?'

'Now, about that...' I begin. Then taking my courage in both hands: 'I'm quitting.'

'Erm... *what* did you say?'

'I'm quitting.'

'You're kidding me!'

'No I'm not.'

'What are you, a journalist or something? That's happened before: some halfwit went through the initiation and then wrote it all up for the papers.'

'No, I'm not a journalist.'

Nils frowns.

'Really—you're not?'

'Really.'

Nils scratches his head.

'Okay... I'm baffled. Why?'

I take a deep breath.

'Well, one thing has been made very clear during this week: if you are a member of the fraternity, you are someone. Being a member here means being someone.'

'And... so?' He looks at me in total bewilderment.

'Well, I don't want to be the kind of person you're all pretending to be here.'

'Jesus, Novitius, have you totally lost your mind during the last two weeks? I know the initiation is tough, but our goal isn't to actually send people crazy. Have you gone crazy, Novitius?'

'No I haven't, Nils.' I pause. 'I'm quitting. This is as far as I go. I'm off. Thanks for an interesting fortnight.'

'Okay, Novitius, goodbye then.'

Nils stares at me, then his puzzled frown morphs into a look of utter determination.

'If you are a journalist, Novitius, we will totally completely fucking destroy you.'

'Relax, man! Thanks, but I'm not a journalist. Goodbye.'

2. La douce France

Sweet France.

'Well, a bit too sweet for me,' I think, looking down a toilet filled with vomit from what had once been chocolate éclairs. 'How the hell did this happen?'

It all started with thoughts. Everybody knows them, those voices in your head, those words that keep prattling on while you lie in bed at night. People who think out loud are labelled lunatics or schizophrenics, but everybody talks to themselves all the time, because everybody has the story of their 'I' fixed firmly in their head.

Instead of learning how to calm our minds in puberty, our upbringing and education encourage us from an early age to think all the time. And by focusing our attention on our thoughts, we accumulate a lot of tension—which leads to even more thoughts.

My way to get rid of that tension was running, a lot of running. Ten kilometres a day. Twenty kilometres at week-ends. Day after day. Running until I was completely empty of thoughts and could sleep like a baby.

It took me another five years to find out that you can calm your mind by focusing your attention on your body, by bringing your attention down into your body, really feeling it.

Running was my own personal distraction, but everyone has their little neurotic obsessions to keep thoughts under control: gardening, eating, drinking, working, smoking, controlling, chatting, Facebook, masturbation. It all comes down to the same thing: avoiding the real issue, which is asking yourself why you are doing these things in the first place.

In my case, that realisation was yet to happen.

Every action has a reaction, and all this running led to a nagging pain which, after four years, developed into a serious knee problem, until I started to think that I had probably permanently damaged the cartilage. I tried to ignore the problem, hoping that, if I kept on running, it would disappear by itself. Needless to say, that didn't work. Running was part of who I was. Without the running I lost control over who I was, and the sleepless nights returned. The only solution was to keep on running. And so I was still running a shitload.

Anyway, after saying goodbye to Nils, I had arrived in 'la douce France': to learn French, to eat well, to enjoy French culture. After an ultra-long running session, my hunger had been so intense that I'd eaten six éclairs in quick succession. *Bam!* A real sugar bomb. Not a good idea. Hence the toilet filled with vomit.

A crossroads had been reached: running no longer made sense. In short, the 'being someone' was starting to wobble—just a little, but it was starting to wobble. Just as it wobbles for everyone once in a while. And funnily enough, I was quite happy about that.

3. But sir... we are thinking here

'They're thinking,' my guide told me.

'What about?' I ask.

'Complicated things... erm... geopolitics, international law, that sort of thing.'

'Do you mind if I look around for a bit? I promise I won't disturb anyone.'

'Well, okay, go ahead. You've got half an hour.'

'Thanks.'

I enter a large room of dark leather sofas surrounded on all sides by shelves filled with books. At every corner there are a couple of computers, and everywhere students and older men are bent over their books, deep in thought.

This is Oxford, the Faculty of International Relations and International Law to be precise, and specifically the Faculty's reading room for professors and PhD students.

I like Oxford. It's traditional, quiet; it has a nice vibe about it. It seems like a good place to improve my English and think about future study plans.

But even though this room is quite stunning—full of fascinating books, beautiful furniture and antique paintings—one thing is very noticeable: the people in it are not happy. Frowning foreheads, wrinkled faces, greasy skin, dark rings around the eyes, probably caused by years of lack of sleep and a shortage of vitamins.

A feeling of heaviness comes over me as I focus my attention on the people in this room. For the first time, I am observing people from another perspective, really looking at them, really feeling them. There is a lot of thinking going on in this room, that's for sure, but it certainly doesn't look as though the thinking is making these people happy.

After half an hour the man who had let me in comes over to me with a wink, and I walk rapidly towards the exit.

Half an hour was more than enough, because there was only one true feeling in that room: pain. A room full of pain.

While I walk through the nearby park, I see two kids playing in the sand, full of joy and laughter, their mothers watching quietly to the side.

Thinking—a lot of thinking—is unnatural. The constant battle in our head weighs the mind down and has its repercussions on the body. From frowning professors to joyful kids. The contrast is so overwhelming that one particular thought comes quickly to the forefront of my mind: thinking does not make for happiness.

There is nothing wrong with thinking in general. The mind likes to play with thoughts. But a lot of thinking hurts, especially when the thinking is aimed at adding 'something' to 'yourself', at 'being someone'.

It's our identification with and emotional attachment to language and form, our need to be 'someone', which leads to all the forceful thinking, to the mental 'I': the voice which every human being knows so well, that voice which everyone claims as 'my own thoughts'.

The 'I' itself is a thought, a thought from which one derives one's identity, and it is exactly that 'I' which leads us from one extreme—joyful children—to the other—frowning professors.

We feel trapped and lonely and cannot stand to be alone, because we are separated from everything by our identification with a mentally created sense of self, the ego, the 'I-identity'.

'What is that "I"? If "I" is just a thought in my head, who is it who is watching the "I"?' I ponder. 'How can "I" have thoughts?'

Since I'd no longer been able to keep up my daily runs, sleepless nights had followed one after another. I had quickly found another way to avoid the thinking: biking, hundreds of kilometres of biking across the English countryside. (I also ate very little, because I'd realised that the mind slows down when it doesn't have a lot of energy to burn. Obviously, I lost quite a lot of weight.)

My mind is racing, and so I quickly jump on my bike and start distracting myself all over again.

Without realising it, I had briefly touched upon the question addressed by all serious philosophical and spiritual traditions: Who am 'I'?

4. A pancake on the Waal, straightforward

'I'd like one of those pancakes, please.'

'Here, enjoy it!' says the cheerful man in the pancake shop, handing me a paper-wrapped bundle.

'Thanks,' I say, quickly taking a warm bite from the top. Hmmm... so good.

I go and sit on a bench and look out over the River Waal in Nijmegen.

'Fuck! What a shitty day... hardcore suffering,' I mumble to myself.

◎ ◎ ◎

'If you study law, then it's straightforward,' the professor told us during our first class. 'You have to get used to sleeping no more than seven hours a night. You can't lie in bed for ten hours straight. This is about work, work and more work, and only then can you achieve what I have achieved.'

Professor De Vught's face is getting redder by the minute.

'Jesus, he's going to explode!' says the girl next to me and, before I know it, I'm laughing out loud.

'What are you laughing at?' yells Professor De Vught, becoming redder still. 'Just wait! You'll see! Law is no laughing matter. It's the core of existence. Without law there can be no society!'

'I agree that society needs a certain degree of order,' I interject. 'Anarchy really doesn't work. But the core of existence—isn't that taking things a bit too far?'

'No, it's not! Law is crucial, essential, profound!'

'Oh, okay. Sorry!'

◎ ◎ ◎

Luckily I was starting to get to know myself better, and I realised pretty quickly that this was not the way forward. The core of existence—law? I just couldn't get it.

The result was immediate: my mind started going wild again. I quit studying and was reduced once more to a 'nobody', because the idea that I was going to become 'someone' through studying had collapsed. There followed a lot of unrest, a bit of depression, and in my desperation I tried to work in an office for a while, but that wasn't the solution either.

Strange as it may seem, at one level I enjoyed the failure because, if you make mistakes, if you fail, life is showing you that the path you're on is not the way forward. So at least I knew in which direction *not* to go. I was finally able to admit to myself that not knowing what I wanted was not a bad thing if I could embrace the not-knowing. Honesty: that's the important thing, and I was starting to appreciate honesty a lot.

Even though everything seemed to be messed up—no more studying, barely any friends left, as I stared out over the River Waal I realised that life had become nicely straightforward, in that at least it was showing me what not to do.

5. Girls have sex with their asses in the mud

'You've never left the village? You're joking!'

'No I'm not,' says Gert.

He goes on: 'I've never ever left the village. Why would I? It's awesome here! Nice work... drinking beer... And once a year we have this huge party tent out on a farm. Incredible, man! Girls get completely hammered and willingly have sex there with their asses in the mud.'

'I don't believe you,' I say, my mouth open.

Gert and I are working in the backyard of a mansion in the village I grew up in. We're tearing down a tree.

'If you're not going to study, then you have to work' had been my orders from home. And when I started gardening, I soon came to realise that being in nature is actually quite relaxing; it's nice and calm. However, there was still a sense of restlessness, an itching inside: there *must* be more to life than gardening. Not that being a gardener is bad—it's a great job.

'So what do you do in your free time?' I ask Gert.

'Well, drink beer... you know... watch porn.'

'Beer drinking I know,' I answer, 'and watching porn— who hasn't watched porn? Who hasn't masturbated?'

We continue working on the tree.

'So what are you going to do with your life?' asks Gert after a while.

'I don't know. Maybe study again.'

'Studying—ah, man! Why would you do that? You don't need that!'

'To get out of the village, maybe I do need to study.'

'But why? Why leave the village?' asks Gert.

'Well... good question! In all honesty, I have no idea.'

But deep down I did know. I'd felt since I was young that there had to be more to life.

The restlessness, the sleepless nights, got so bad that one day I sat on my bike on my way to work and just started crying... That was enough: staying in the village was also not the way to go.

'I'll go back to studying,' I thought. 'Why not?'

If I'd learned one thing, it was that honesty is crucial, especially honesty towards yourself. However, whilst I was definitely being honest at that time, there was no focus at all on the key question: 'Who am I?'

Nevertheless, although for much of the time I wasn't clearly conscious of it, the question was still alive and, luckily, continued to emerge once in a while. And bit by bit, something deep down was nurturing it.

6. 1.5 litres of beer for five euro... burndepression

'Life can't get better than this,' I think, waking up next to a girl in a big bed in a room on a student campus. The evening before we'd done hallucinogenic mushrooms with ten friends. Interesting things, these mushrooms—definitely worth trying at least once in your life.

The university college where I'm enrolled is also interesting, mainly because of the social life. Five euro buys you 1.5 litres of beer in the local bar, and student life is one big party. Beer, beer, beer, lots of beer.

There's a word for this: 'denial'. Most people are totally unconscious of the fact that they're unconscious, that they're totally identified with their 'I'-identity. Unconsciousness means being trapped within your own mental boundaries without being aware of it.

Denial has many forms, and humanity is good at finding ways to channel this denial: war, violence, hatred, entertainment, drinking, drugs—all the forms of distraction you can think of.

Distraction arises out of fear, the fear of really looking at the emptiness behind the 'I'. And that fear in essence is a terror of being alone, of not being 'someone'—because being truly alone means no longer receiving the confirmation that you are 'someone'. A couple of days or even hours alone in a room without distraction is, for most people, sheer hell.

Luckily, I had enough distractions on campus, and hence was totally unconscious and deep in denial. But under the surface, the experiences of the previous years were simmering and, where there is simmering, there will at some point come a boiling over. After a year and a half of joyfully intense student life, the exhaustion which had accumulated in my mind and body was starting to have its effect, and boil over it all did.

Every great change or challenge in life results in stress, and since I had already been subject to quite a few of these changes, my mind and body were exhausted.

There was, besides, the hard partying of student life, and a girlfriend who kept me active late into the night.

One night I awoke, shaking in my bed, and I thought, 'Jesus, what's going on now?'

The shaking didn't go away, and the following years were spent in a state of total unrest. I went through all the symptoms of stress, burnout, depression, hormonal imbalance, anxiety. I went to loads of doctors, and the horror of it all went on for two and a half years non-stop.

I tried to use the pain to educate and heal myself, step by step. After shaking for weeks on end, I read that it must be caused by a shortage of magnesium. And the bloating, diarrhoea and stomach pains I was experiencing must have something to do with my diet. So I radically changed my eating habits. I also tried to sleep loads, because that did seem to alleviate the feeling of burnout. Heart palpitations were a daily occurrence, so I applied heart coherence techniques. I then read that the feeling of 'dying', brought about by panic attacks, was linked to low carbon dioxide levels in the blood, so I trained myself to breathe slowly from my abdomen instead of my previous rapid superficial breathing. My diarrhoea was remedied through stomach massages, and my feelings of depression lessened by Chinese acupressure.

I had never really believed in energy healing and that sort of thing until I visited an acupuncturist in Amsterdam. He inserted twelve needles into my body, and I started shaking intensely for half an hour. Thirty minutes later I felt better than I'd ever felt before: like a baby, reborn, so relaxed. After that experience I started educating myself in acupuncture and acupressure, and also trained myself in some Taoist techniques after a few tips from a therapist.

In essence, *chi* (also called *prana* in India or 'life force' in the west; many other terms are used in different cultures) is a real phenomenon, but you only really believe that once you have consciously experienced it, just as you only really believe that alcohol makes you drunk once you've been drunk.

Some might argue that chi is purely a subjective phenomenon. That doesn't make it any less real, though. Feelings and emotions, for example, are also subjective phenomena, but nobody denies their existence. Everybody knows also that dreams exist, although nobody has ever been able to prove the existence of a dream scientifically.

Having said which, it can, of course, be argued that the existence of dreams can, to an extent, be objectively proven: when someone's under an MRI scan, you can see parts of the brain light up during those moments in which they are dreaming. And it's also true to say that, if, for example, you can deliberately direct a lot of chi to your hands and feet when under an infrared scan, whole areas of the body light up.

The reason that most people do not believe in the existence of chi is that most people are never calm enough to become conscious of it. If you want to feel chi, you have to be calm, really calm.

The main exercise I practised was as follows: I sat down, closed my eyes and focused on my navel. Every time I caught myself thinking, I directed my attention back to my navel. Gradually my mind became totally calm. And after a couple of weeks of doing this exercise for fifteen minutes a day, I started to feel a sort of warm ball in the navel area. After a while I could send this 'warm ball' around my body, which was a wonderful feeling. I read a lot about these Taoist techniques, which were made accessible in the west by Mantak Chia, who has created a system of meditations, massage techniques and exercises. But the first step is always this navel exercise because, first, you have to *feel* the chi.

And I was going to end up really needing these techniques, because suddenly my health got a lot worse ...

'Well, Tim, we've done the investigations now, and I'm afraid we don't have very good news for you,' says Dr van Putten.

'What's the matter then?'

'There are cells in your small intestine which are overactive—hyperplastic we call it—and your body is being continuously bombarded with hormones. That's why your symptoms have been getting worse. I don't know if your previous stress symptoms are linked to this, because something like this builds up over years. The hormones could be the cause of your symptoms, but your behaviour in the past might in itself have encouraged overactive cellular activity.'

'That's probably true,' I tell him. 'I've not looked after my body over the past couple of years... I've gone through some pretty tough times.'

Dr van Putten looks down at his charts.

'In any case,' he says, after a moment, 'we must just hope that it won't get any worse. We're not going to have to give you chemotherapy—it's not full-blown cancer yet. We call it carcinoid syndrome. It's at a very early stage, so we'll keep an eye on it. I'll see you every six months.'

'Great,' I think, 'cancer—that's all I need! Life sucks!'

But I immediately take a decision: 'I'm going to get better, no matter what, and no matter what anyone else thinks.'

And thanks to the Taoist techniques, that goal is accomplished. With the aid of a long list of books, I change my lifestyle radically: no meat, no alcohol, little animal protein, loads of fruit, vegetables, smoothies, nuts, seeds, superfoods, etc. In addition, I do hundreds or even thousands of hours of a Taoist meditation which aims at dissolving energetic imbalances in the body.

'So how are you feeling, Tim?' asks Dr van Putten at my first six-monthly check-up.

'Well… tired,' I say.

'Yes, your 5-HIAA hormonal levels are still way too high. Are you sure you don't want treatment?'

'No—absolutely not,' I reply.

I keep on with the meditation. I feel that the imbalance in my stomach area is getting less, as if the energy is starting to flow again.

At the next check-up, the same sort of conversation happens.

'So... your 5-HIAA levels are still too high. We really ought to do something about that,' says Dr van Putten.

'No, I'd rather die,' I reply. 'I don't believe that a chemical bombardment can heal a body that's already sick.'

With the possibility of premature death hanging over me, there is obviously a huge incentive to pour serious attention into exploring techniques to heal the body with chi. And the Taoist techniques improve my health so much that, after three check-ups, my hormone levels are back to normal.

Dr van Putten says: 'I don't know exactly what you've been doing, but whatever it is, keep on doing it!'

He also briefly mentions the fact that there are many medical mysteries which western science cannot explain, and that certain eastern meditation techniques can have a profound effect on the body. Dr van Putten is, in fact, a pretty open-minded doctor—cool!

◎ ◎ ◎

The first major step in my own healing process had been to read Mantak Chia's *Awakening healing energy through the Tao*. This is an excellent introduction to the Taoist energy teachings on chi, which are incredibly effective in restoring the entire human organism to healthy functioning. Taoists—and consequently acupuncturists—have known for millennia that cancer is caused by energetic imbalances in the body. Dealing with these imbalances at an early stage is a way of preventing the development of cancer and, if practised vigorously, also a way of getting rid of it.

And in my case it had worked.

I'm not saying that the Taoist techniques will always heal cancer, but it's highly unlikely that cancer will manifest in someone who is trained in these techniques... unless they're subject to something like a nuclear holocaust, of course.

The ancient Taoist wisdom encompasses one of the clearest and most advanced systems for dealing with the physical, mental and energetic development and healing of a human being, and Mantak Chia has done a superb job in making it available in the west. He has, moreover, made available a mass of useful knowledge on natural healing, from eye exercises which enable those with defective sight to dispense with their glasses, to learning how to recycle sexual energy, to advanced medical *chi gong* and a lot more. (For further information, look into Mantak Chia's Taoist universal healing system.)

Through developing the ability to feel and balance energy, one basically transcends all the principles of western psychology in one fell swoop. And even a psychologist or philosopher who has studied their discipline for decades and decades, should they actually experience chi energy, will realise the futility of their previous thought-based efforts.

There have, of course, been many famous psychologists and philosophers who were not familiar with the energetic practices of Taoism because, while the *Tao Te Ch'ing* and *I Ching* have long been available in the west, it's only in the last forty years that Mantak Chia, a Taoist himself, has made these carefully guarded secrets easily accessible.

I must stress, however, that these practices cannot be understood just by reading philosophical texts: they can only be truly understood through dedicated practice. Thanks to the wisdom of Chinese medicine based on the teachings of the Taoist masters, tens of thousands of people are now using these techniques to radically improve their health. You can choose yourself how far you want to go: from simply meditating as a way of calming the mind, to restoring your organs to full health, to meditating alone in a dark cave.

In time, western psychology will come to acknowledge their importance, simply because they are so effective. The fact that science, psychology, philosophy—in short, the entire edifice of western knowledge—does not even recognise chi shows how undeveloped our western way of life still is.

Pain has a way of confronting you with your limits. You can hide in fixed behavioural patterns and deny the pain, or you can admit it to yourself and use it as a guide to develop and challenge yourself. Embrace pain and suffering, observe it, learn from it, because it is telling you something is wrong, and that makes it a gift.

Nothing is as difficult for a human being to grasp as new ideas, but once you have experienced chi, once you have really felt it, you will never forget it.

Chi is the link between the physical world of the senses and the emptiness out of which all flows. Diving into that emptiness is what true spirituality is about but, if you want to develop yourself step by step, or heal yourself from a serious illness, then learning about chi is a great way to do it.

7. Finally

'Hey Tim, have you ever thought about what reality is and who we really are? Whether we're not just fooling ourselves about who we are?'

'Yes, yes, yes, yes, yes!' I reply. 'Of course! But I never realised other people think about it too.'

'Well, I have a book here which I think you should read. It's about spiritual enlightenment. It's pretty intense, but it's also quite clear on the subject.'

'Thanks, man—thanks a lot! It's incredible that you've been thinking along the same lines. I've never talked about it with anyone.'

After receiving my first book on spirituality from my best friend Michael, I quickly started ordering more. I especially enjoyed reading the ones that really make you think and question everything at the most fundamental of levels.

For example, if your 'I', your image of yourself, is what you think you are, if you think you are your name, how do you actually see the thought 'I', your self-image, your name in your mind?

Think about it.

Close your eyes and ask yourself: 'Who am I?'

If the answer is 'I am me', who is it who is watching the thought 'I am me'?

Try again. If the 'I' is what you think you are, what is conscious of the 'I'?

What is 'I' anyway?

Are words what I am? Can I define myself through language, feelings, experiences?

To truly figure out what you are—and what you are not, to find out the truth behind the 'I' and everything else: that is the essence of the struggle for enlightenment.

◎ ◎ ◎

'Finally, finally, finally… there's a way to break through,' I thought as I lay in bed. At last I was starting to realize that what I thought I was, was not really what I am. My reading had also taught me that there is a way to break through all the fixed ideas and mental patterns which make up this 'I-identity', the ego.

This was what, deep down, I had been looking for all along. This is why I had rejected everything, why I was always unconsciously pushing myself to my limits. In essence, I was looking for a final way out of my own suffering, the suffering generated by the 'I-identity'.

During this period, different aspects of self-enquiry became clear pretty quickly. For instance, every time I started thinking about breaking away from the 'I-identity', I realised that I was also looking for confirmation of my existence by clinging to my emotional attachments (to people, ideas, concepts, feelings, trains of thought, thoughts of the future, friends, hobbies, etc). And I soon saw that the process of breaking away just couldn't continue so long as I was holding on to these attachments.

Stimulated by thinking and suffering, I was beginning to

question the whole way I functioned, for the more we think and suffer, the more likely it is that we start to question. That's why pain, as I said, can be such a tremendous gift.

The 'I-identity', though, is like a rubber band: it won't snap if I just let it be. I have to stretch it to its limits for it finally to break. I had to be on my guard, because playing with a rubber band could be so much fun that I could spend my whole life toying with it without stretching it to breaking point.

Meditating a couple of times a week, for example, is nice and cosy, but it's not going to get you to the final boundary. Neither will being mindful for a few hours a week. Attempting to build yourself a 'spiritual' identity, to use spirituality to avoid suffering, will also never work: trying to convince yourself intellectually that all is 'just emptiness' or 'just a dream' is plain foolish as well.

In fact, even the most detailed in-depth conceptual understanding of the fundamentals of Advaita, Zen, Taoism, Buddhism, Non-duality, Yoga, Christian Mysticism/Hermeticism, Daism, Sufism, Theosophy, Transcendentalism, Rosicrucianism, Kabbalah, Kashmir Shaivism, Shamanism, Tibetan Buddhist Dzogchen, Parapsychology or any other spiritual, philosophic or esoteric tradition is never going to lead to a dismantling of the 'I-identity'. I had studied and researched all these spiritual traditions at one time or another, but the struggle for enlightenment is not about entrenching yourself deeper in thoughts and concepts.

Equally, retreating into the spiritual swamp of vague, new-age teachings, flitting from one teacher to another, opening a beautiful spiritual centre, inviting famous spiritual teachers to talk there, reading spiritual quotes every day, reading book after book about the nature of experience and non-duality... It became clear to me that all of this would be in vain if it didn't eventually lead to the realisation that you can only *really* figure it out by taking radical action, in solitude.

Combining a modern active life in the 'normal' world with an honest and committed quest for enlightenment simply doesn't work, and my attempt to 'have a foot in both camps' would end up almost ripping me apart in conflict and frustration. When I finally got it totally clear in my mind that I was fooling myself with my belief in the 'I-identity', I realised that a huge transformation was in the making.

Whilst I was pondering over all this, I also began to deepen my understanding of all the different kinds of human behaviour that can be seen on this planet. Everyone is looking for themselves in their own way: from 'the cool guy in the village' roaring around in his customized car, to money-crazed bankers, to those on spiritual retreats and a quest for 'self-exploration'. This is a society, however, where turning inward is basically taboo, and no matter how insane human behaviour gets, as long as everyone is doing it, that's fine, because everybody agrees that nothing is worse than being all alone and having nothing to do. Whilst all may seem very pleasant on their multi-million-dollar luxury super yachts, even a billionaire cannot be alone without distractions for very long without their thoughts driving them crazy.

And if the quest for possessions was really going to make people happy, then the 20th and 21st centuries would be the happiest period in the history of humanity, because never have we had it so good.

Obviously, this isn't the case. So this grand human experiment can now be definitively concluded: the quest for possessions doesn't bring happiness. So instead of looking outside, let's have a look inside.

So I began with questions like:

- What am I looking for?

- Who is the one looking?

- What do I do to find out what I really am or what I am not?

- Who in the past seems to have found out how to be truly honest with themselves, and how did they go about it?

If you look at history, you can observe that all awakened men and women have gone through a period of isolation prior to a radical awakening and the deconstruction of the 'I-identity'. During their struggle for awakening, what they've had in common is that they have chosen solitude, not yielding to the pressures of society, and they have been willing to take radical action. Take, for example, the Sufi master Mansur Al Hallaj, who kept repeating 'I am the absolute truth', even when they were cutting off his arms, his legs and other body parts, one by one, for his so-called heresy.

The 'I-identity'—what you think of as yourself—will do anything to survive, and only radical measures have a chance of success. The 'I'-identity' can be super smart, so don't underestimate the challenge this presents.

While many books never even mention it, sexual energy is obviously a major driving force in human beings. Sexual and domestic violence, the prostitution business and other forms of sexual madness and exploitation can only be prevented if we teach ourselves and others how to feel, balance and recycle sexual energy.

But just as with everything else, you have to figure this out for yourself.

There are lots of different points of view on the topic. Taoists say you can have sex as long as you recycle the sexual energy. Some Buddhists say you shouldn't have sex at all. Some yogis do tantra, while others practise total abstinence. A transcendentalist might urge you to go beyond sex, whilst a Sufi master would explain it all in a totally different way. One famous Zen master spent his life in a brothel, whilst another lived alone in the forest and probably never got his dick up at all. And then a Jew might urge you to get your dick circumcised. Some say it's all about being in 'the now' during sex—others insist that sexual energy should catapult you beyond the physical plane into higher spiritual realms and advanced states of consciousness.

If you study Chinese medicine, Taoism, Ayurveda and the human body in general for a while, you will soon enough realise that conserving sexual energy has tremendous benefits for your physical and energetic well-being. There is obviously a good reason why true spiritual masters practise celibacy, because transcending the 'I-identity' without transcending the need for sex is impossible. It is also understandable, from an energetic point of view, why the church still promotes celibacy in the clergy.

However, simply telling people to be celibate or to practise sexual restraint without teaching them how to do it is like trying to divert a river without digging a canal. The result is repressed sexual energy, which eventually finds its way out in the form of all kinds of sexual perversions and scandals, often involving supposedly spiritual people. Blocking the river of sexual energy by building a mental dam will never work, for eventually the dam will overflow. The real key lies in teaching people how to transform their sexual energy.

I am familiar through personal experience with the effectiveness of the Taoist practices of cultivating and transforming male sexual energy (see *Taoist secrets of love*, or *The multi-orgasmic man*). There are Taoist energy techniques for women as well (see *Healing love through the Tao*, or *The multi-orgasmic woman*). Women who have trained themselves in these techniques can, for example, drastically reduce the amount of blood they lose during their period. And by conserving these fluids, they can conserve a great deal of energy.

Women can also learn to protect themselves from the aggressive stare of the male. It's something that can be seen on busy streets in every society: women who quickly lower their heads when confronted by a man's gaze. Everything in the world is connected, so if a man looks at a woman with a certain thought or intention, most women pick this up intuitively. They know what it means, and can feel really threatened by the 'I want to mate with you' message inherent in the stare. Nevertheless, only a rare few know how to properly protect themselves from this 'bad' energy.

Basic Taoist energy practices are an excellent way of creating energetic protection through raising the level of chi in the body, while the more advanced practices establish a form of protection which is permanent. For both women and men, Taoist energy practices are a treasure house of useful information regarding the physical, mental and energetic development of a human being.

Beware, however, because working with energy can in itself form a huge distraction, so let's apply some focus.

Before embarking on the struggle for awakening, or when you are already engaged in the struggle, you might want to educate yourself as to how best to deal with the power of sexual energy. As I said earlier, one can observe that all those who have truly struggled for enlightenment have gone through a radical process of awakening and a long period of isolation. During their struggle, they were alone; during this period, they didn't have sex. And once you know, for example, how to recycle sexual energy using Taoist techniques, it's a lot easier to sustain concentration and commitment when you're not being distracted by a boner in your pants or some serious wetness between your legs.

What happens after the struggle is over... well... then you won't have to worry about anything anyway.

So yes, you do have to figure it out for yourself, but don't underestimate the power of sexual energy and the grip it can exert on the 'I-identity'.

And what about love in all of this? Tranquillity, non-attachment, total openness, compassion and many other qualities might all manifest after the 'I-identity' has been taken apart.

If I were simply to say things like: 'Love is all... just feel the love... be the love... love the "I-identity"... be totally open... feel the loving energy running like a river through your body... dissolve everything in love... be the one true loving non-dual transcendental consciousness', nothing would ever happen. All the love talk is simply a distraction from finding out what the 'I' really is. These instructions wouldn't even make sense to most people, since most human beings have a tremendous resistance to life, which is the antithesis of love.

What most people call love is, in any case, nothing more than the tendency for separate 'I-identities' to 'feed' on each other because, on their own, they feel so incomplete. If you feel incomplete, if your 'cup is not full', do not feed on other people. Don't start having children to 'fill your cup'. Having a relationship, or having children, should be an expression of abundance—not an act of poverty. These things should happen when your cup is overflowing—not when it's half-empty.

Moreover, it is not through the cultivation of qualities like love and compassion that the 'I-identity' will collapse. On the contrary, the attempt to enhance such qualities will result in a cultivation that can only be temporary and that will need continual, effortful reinforcement. In short, it will only make the 'I-identity' stronger.

If there is one common denominator in human behaviour, it is that humans only change when things get really tough. Whether on a personal or a global level, human beings— human societies—only change profoundly when confronted with crisis, great suffering or death.

An important facet in the process of true self-enquiry is to put yourself into situations so tough that you are willing to pay any price to get out of them. If you shove a peaceful dog or cat into a corner, it turns violent: it wants to get out of that situation at any cost. The spiritual search is similar. Once you really put yourself into the corner, once you start to understand what a prison the 'I-identity' really is, the 'I-identity' will fight with all it's got to stay alive. Then you realise what a tough battle this is going to be, since you have to go into that corner and strangle the cornered dog (the 'I-identity') with your bare hands—over and over again. And the dog will attack you, scratch you, bite you or—more insidiously—pretend to be so at peace that you really do not want to fight with it anymore.

In real Zen there are three essential ingredients for enlightenment: faith that enlightenment is possible, an intense questioning (doubt) of everything, and iron determination. So in order to progress, I made the following clear to myself: I am in denial, I do not know who I am or what is true; and to confront that, I have to really focus, in solitude. If I don't focus on that with my entire being, I'm just fooling myself, because living life pretending to know who I am is a complete waste of time.

8. Metal worms full of monkeys

'Tsjjjjjjjjjjjjjjjjjjjjjjj ...pieeeeeep!'

The metal worm slowly comes to a standstill. Hundreds of people storm out on to the platform at Waterloo Station. A warm, humid, unhealthy, polluted stream of air immediately slams into my face, the kind of air you only find in subways, and especially in the London subway. One more station to go until I'm home. Home at the moment is a student house in the centre of London, situated at a crossroads where hundreds of buses pass by every hour, a veritable Valhalla of toxic fumes and especially diesel fumes, the most carcinogenic ones.

The subway is so crowded that my face has been pushed up against a window. Everybody's comfort zone has been invaded, if not completely overwhelmed.

'Two more minutes to go,' I think to myself. 'Stay calm, stay calm... breathe deeply!'

'Brrrrrrrrr... bammmmmmmmmmmm!'

With a great bang the train suddenly comes to a halt in the middle of the tunnel. I look out of the window and see that there's about thirty centimetres to the side of the tunnel.

'Fuck, fuck, fuck.'

After half an hour without moving, the temperature in the train has risen significantly. Some are almost fainting, and there is a minor degree of panic.

Luckily, we start to move again and we arrive at the station two minutes later. Everybody sighs with relief.

The moment I get home, I go straight to bed. This has become a pattern for me over the past couple of weeks: lying in bed, suffering, thinking, meditating, more suffering, going for walks, sitting for a couple of hours a day in a jacuzzi.

When you start to ponder about the 'I-identity', you open yourself up to previously unimagined possibilities, so this struggle also entails a radical new learning process. Education and information on all subjects has basically become freely available thanks to the internet, which is truly great if you want to educate yourself. However, there is also the danger of an overkill of information, so maintaining focus is important. This is easier said than done, because once you start shaking it at its fundamentals, the 'I-identity' strikes back a hundred times harder than ever before.

After I'd finished my bachelor degree in Utrecht, it became clearer and clearer that I was fooling myself with my belief in the 'I' and, as a consequence, the 'I-identity' started to pull out all its tricks to stay in control: 'Yes, but you need a career'... 'Yes, but without money you can't survive'... 'If you get a masters in economics, you'll be able to earn a lot of money quickly on the stock market—then you can *really* start going for the enlightenment thing'. I even went to a therapist, who also tried to convince me that studying was the only way forward. I walked straight into these mental traps and, before I knew it, I was in a classroom full of students who were convinced that the only way to make it in life was to become rich.

Every thought, every emotion, every feeling, every idea will be used by the 'I-identity' to convince you not to try to deconstruct it.

33

So I went to London, where I stumbled from one mental trap into another: denial, followed by a 'fuck-it-all' attitude, back to denial again, to a weird kind of 'accept-it-all' attitude, then back to denial again.

Since I'd begun reading spiritual and philosophical books and really thinking about the question of the 'I-identity', I'd been travelling for around a year and a half through these cycles of denial, while trying to combine two things that are just about impossible to combine: the quest for awakening and life in the 'normal' world.

The 'I-identity' ruled supreme at this time... leaving me a sad alienated clown.

As I said earlier, our whole society is focused on the denial of introspection. And if you have the guts to truly question yourself, the herd is quick to judge you: 'Why think about these things?'... 'Why can't you be "normal" like the rest of us?'... 'Just be yourself—be happy!'... 'Of course my mind and body are me!'

Other people's 'I-identities' will always try to convince you not to start shaking the foundations of the 'I-identity', because nothing is scarier for people than to see someone confronting the fears they dare not confront themselves. Consequently, the search to find out who you really are may lead to massive criticism from the people around you. A decent upbringing, education, studying... and for what? To become a slave in a society where the highest goal is to acquire a lot of useless things; to do some useless job, build up a sizable figure in your bank account—which you can then spend on holidays and acquiring more material things. No thanks—fuck that.

Soon I had dropped out of university and, because of this

struggle with the 'I-identity', my health deteriorated. I would spent days walking around London and sitting in subways observing the human condition—principally, of course, my own misery.

One afternoon I found myself sitting in a jacuzzi, where even the warm bubbles could no longer relax me. I walked back home and thought, 'If I don't focus properly on all this right now, I'll kill myself.' That thought led to total panic: 'Jesus, this is going too far!'

After years of physical and mental madness—the destructive running, the cycling, the swimming, the burn-out, depression and unrest born of stress, and now this spiritual madness I was experiencing in London—I'd had enough. I'd been at war with myself for so long already that I'd come to the point where I was willing to make the ultimate effort.

I left London, the relationship with my girlfriend broke apart—and I finally realised that this was about one thing only: the final boundary.

9. Destruction

Over and over again I focused the mind on the same question: 'What is the "I"?' The thoughts kept bouncing round my head. And time and again I took apart every answer my mind produced. Every thought, feeling, idea, concept arises and passes in the mind, hence they can be observed and discarded as not being 'me'. How otherwise could I observe them?

Months I spent like this, living in Nicaragua. Not that Nicaragua particularly interested me, but it was warm, cheap and super calm. I went for long walks on abandoned beaches, jumped in the ocean once in a while, but most of the time I was focusing my mind and struggling with the 'I-identity': 'If I can observe my "I", then that is not what "I" am'... 'If the world is perception, it is not absolutely true' ...

The dissolution of emotional attachments is an essential part of this struggle. Emotions: e-motions. Energy motions: motions of energy. Positive and negative motions of energy. Attachments through which the 'I-identity' keeps itself alive.

Emotional attachments can be dissolved either by concentrating intensely on them in meditation, or by bringing them into focus through a writing process combined with meditation. These two processes slowly dissolve the attachments of the 'I-identity' by freeing up the emotional energy that sustains them. Some prefer to write everything down, others prefer to do it in their head. I did it in my head.

I spent days and days, for example, looking at a fork until

my mind stopped calling it a fork and there was no longer a question of a fork having any real existence. Then I spent weeks just observing bodily feelings, until I realised that the whole body is simply a perception. And how therefore could there be an 'I' inhabiting this so-called body? Alan Watts describes it nicely when he says: 'The way of liberation is a progressive disentanglement of one's "I" from every identification.' A process of 'unknowing' what you always thought you knew for sure. A process of taking apart every single belief you think is true.

I remember reading that it's important for people to know that liberation or enlightenment is possible, that there is a way out of suffering which will result in a state of absolute liberation: the complete dissolution of the physical, mental, energetic and spiritual projection you have of yourself.

I carried on like this for a long time, exhausted and frustrated from fighting with the 'I-identity', until my consciousness was focusing so intensely on itself that, for a couple of days, I found myself in a kind of weird half-psychotic state.

A few days later I walked, completely drained of energy, to the little restaurant where I ate every day, and something strange happened. The mind calmed down completely. There was nothing to think about anymore, nothing to fight against.

Hundreds of people have tried over the years to describe this state, but I won't do that here. It can't be understood rationally, conceptually or in any other way.

A profound change had occurred, that was for sure... Or at least that seemed to be the case... But we'll come back to that later...

10. Monetary debt-boat

The sound of the water mingles with the chirping of the birds while the leaves blow in the wind, forming a free concert directed by nature. I am steering a little rowing boat around the corner on to the *nieuwe gracht* in Utrecht, a canal which is so small that almost no boats pass through it.

After around five hundred metres, I see a woman sitting by the side of the canal. She has great bags under her eyes. Suddenly she says to me, 'Hey, what a cute little boat!'

'Yes, right,' I say, pulling in to the side.

'How did you get a boat like that?'

'A neighbour lets me borrow it,' I explain. 'If you don't mind my asking, are you all right? You look so tired.'

'Well, actually,' she says, starting to sniffle, 'I'm not right at all!'

And the next thing I know, she's burst into tears.

I try to reassure her: 'Just relax, I'm sure things will be fine.'

'But I'm in so much debt! You have no idea how much!'

'Probably not, but I know that this whole system is based on debt. We're all of us in debt—we're all in the same debt-boat. You're not alone, really!'

'Oh, it's good to hear that!'

We talk for a little longer and then I push off again: 'Enjoy your day!'

◎ ◎ ◎

Living by the canals in Utrecht I spent most days like this. I slept when I wanted, ate when I wanted, walked along the canals at night, made trips in the rowing boat, talked with my housemates and visited my friend Michael.

After I left Nicaragua, I'd lived in Amsterdam for a while, but I quickly realised that functioning in 'normal' society just wasn't possible anymore. Despite my debts, I couldn't pretend to function like a robot and, when I tried, I lasted no more than five minutes: 'Hi, I'm Tim... I can't do this anymore! Bye!'

I ended up in Utrecht again, where I was attempting to deal with some of the side-effects of overcoming the boundaries of the 'I-identity'. Side-effects—what kind of side-effects? Are you telling me that after such a process there are still side-effects? Yes, I'm afraid there are. So what were these side-effects?

Literally a whole new world opened up after the boundaries of the 'I-identity' had been overcome. It was as if the 'I-identity', together with the mind's over-activity, had been blocking my senses and feelings, as if I'd never truly experienced them before. This new sensitivity can be very confusing at the beginning, and it took some time for me to get used to it, to say the least.

The opening up of consciousness leads to direct perception, which gives the ability to look straight through people: all emotions—joy, happiness, fear, pain, suffering—can be perceived instantly. And protecting your energy-field is a handy trick to learn in a world filled with negative energies, whether they be the negative thoughts of fearful 'I-identities', radiation from electronic devices or pollution from mobile networks. When consciousness opens up, there is a huge influx of energy, and the Taoist energetic techniques are excellent ways of learning how to deal with it.

On the positive side, this also means that you immediately know intuitively what is right and wrong, and you act accordingly. This doesn't mean to say that the concepts of 'right' and 'wrong' really mean anything—not at all. Instead, one operates with a heightened sense of intuition rather than in accordance with labels and language. Water knows how to flow by itself, and not being trapped anymore in an 'I-identity' means that you function like a stream. Your 'role' is played out, but you are not really in it: the role is playing itself.

After my conversation with the woman by the canal, I dedicated most of the year to reading books and articles about finance. It wasn't that I felt a deep need to understand it, but I just wanted to clarify for myself the concept of money. There was no longer the stress of trying to figure things out because, when you take apart the 'I-identity' and let go of control in your life, the fear of the unknown totally disappears and you are always open to new ideas.

Money is a concept created by humanity, and money is a force which has exerted a massive influence on human life over the last five thousand years. Money, in short, means debt, and we are all in the same debt-boat.

Money is created by central banks which loan it—with positive interest—to other banks, and the banks loan it—again, with positive interest—to companies and private citizens. (I am using the term 'positive interest' here because, whilst there is also such a thing as negative interest, it isn't relevant to our current growth-based economic system.) Because of the interest payments required by companies and citizens, the money supply has to grow every year, otherwise too many companies and citizens would go broke. And the money supply can only increase every year if the total amount of goods and services produced also increases, otherwise inflation would run out of control.

Inflation is the devaluation of money, due to the increased amount of money available for the same amount of products. To prevent excessive inflation, we need economic growth, so we need to increase the production and consumption of goods and services. We work harder and longer than ever before, despite the fact that, paradoxically, advanced technology was developed so that we could work less.

iPhone 1—throw it away after a year! iPhone 2—throw it away after a year! And on and on. Everyone is familiar with the madness of consumption.

And to keep this interest-based economic system going, we need to use more of the earth's resources—which is leading to the massive devastation of the world's ecosystems and natural resources. Climate change, pollution, the extremes of wealth and poverty, and many other issues of global concern arise from this system. The need for economic growth also translates into a need for the population to keep growing, because we need more consumers to buy more things.

This is a simplified, abbreviated view of the money system—there are, of course, infinite subtleties and complexities—but this is the essence of it. Once you understand that the requirement for positive interest creates the need for cancerous growth, you understand where the destruction of ecosystems and the stratification of rich and poor really begin. Charity, sustainability movements, ecological movements, NGOs, etc—none of these activities can ever lead to a sustainable world, so long as our economic system is based on money with positive interest. And one day, this system will completely collapse, since humanity cannot keep plundering a planet whose resources are finite.

Moreover, in our current system the institutions and people who control the money supply—the banks and the bankers—obviously wield a huge amount of power. Through positive interest, banks make profit on the money which they themselves created out of nothing, and when they cause a financial crisis because of the scandalous way in which they have enriched themselves, ironically, the government bails them out first, because the existence of the banks is so crucial to the system. Quite a clever little scheme the banks have pulled: in essence, it is a form of legalised robbery.

To truly understand the role of money in this way will radically change your view of society. Nothing is wrong with money as a medium of exchange (and nothing is wrong with anything at all once you wake up), but understanding money sheds light on many of the destructive patterns perpetuated by mankind.

So why is it that we are so keen to operate this positive interest-based system in the first place? The requirement for positive interest arises from the requirement of the 'I-identity' to continue experiencing and thus perpetuating itself. The mind is ever in search of more experiences to confirm the existence of the 'I-identity', to perpetuate the illusion of a separate 'me'. Dig deep, and you will see that greed arises from the need to be 'someone': an 'I' who needs more things for 'myself', because without more things 'I' am 'nobody'. In essence, greed arises from our misidentification with who we really are.

As a consequence of being trapped in the 'I-identity', human beings have created an economic system which exacerbates their own mental prisons: people are slaves who are unconsciously perpetuating an economic system which is designed to further enslave them, and to destroy the planet they live on at an ever increasing pace. The combination of the belief in the 'I-identity' with the use of an economic system requiring infinite growth is the main reason why, individually and collectively, we are never at peace and are destroying the planet at such a staggering rate.

In recent times there has been an increase in research into alternative economic systems. I won't go into the details of viable alternatives—you can find that out for yourself (look, for example, into the work of Charles Eisenstein or Bernard Lietaer)—but one day this positive interest-based economic system will be replaced.

To create a truly sustainable society, we would have to change the positive interest-based money system on a global level and, moreover, each of us would have to address the issue of the 'I-identity' on a personal level. But people are so afraid of change—and the economic system is so incredibly intertwined with the belief in the 'I-identity'—that it will probably require an enormous crisis for this to happen.

Imagine a bunch of aliens landing on this planet for the first time. They would wonder why these human monkeys are so anxious, so fearful, so intent on destroying their own home. They would wonder also why the human monkeys consider themselves superior to all the other animals and plants, which seem to be a million times more at ease.

On another planet, our human drama would probably be the most popular comedy/drama show on television: 'Tonight, the show goes on—live monkey madness!'

11. Dead pigs and (s)permaculture

'Disgusting... incredible.' I almost vomit.

Staring at a pile of thirty dead pigs, confronted with the penetrating stench of death, I try to control my retching.

'Are you all right?' asks the French pig farmer.

'Mwoah... just about,' I answer in French.

'Every three days,' the farmer tells me, 'one of them dies. That's why the pile of carcases is so high. But it's all quite normal.'

'Normal!' I mumble to myself. 'Hmm... that's a strange definition of "normal"!'

'Yes,' the farmer continues, 'we keep a couple of thousand pigs here. We have to, to stay competitive.'

The way the economic system functions was pretty clear to me by now so, from a financial point of view, the pressure to keep producing more was logical enough. Hundreds of pigs, all in little metal cages, full of pain and suffering and covered with sores. Funnily enough, the financial system actually encourages practices like this.

'We also have a spermaculture here,' the farmer tells me.

'What's that?' I ask.

'That's where we store the sperm of the male pigs, so that we can create more pigs as quickly as possible.'

'Ah, that makes sense!'

The farmer gives me a look.

'What are you doing here anyway?'

'Oh,' I say, 'I'm staying on a permaculture farm in the neighbourhood.'

'Permaculture—what's that then?' he asks, scratching his head. 'Is it like spermaculture?'

'No, not exactly,' I say. 'Permaculture involves the design and maintenance of agriculturally productive ecosystems which have the resilience, diversity and stability of natural ecosystems.'

'Ahhh,' he says with a smile, 'so you're working with the hippies!'

'Yeah, that's right!' I laugh. 'The people who think the world will end in 2014 when there's a peak in worldwide oil production!'

'They told me about that,' the farmer says, 'but they still expect me to bring them a huge amount of hay every winter with my tractor.'

'Yes, right,' I agree, 'self-sufficiency isn't easy to achieve without using any money at all, unless the life you lead is *really* simple.'

Largely because of widespread ignorance, many people have some very strange habits in regard to nature. For example, people pull out their weeds or, worse still, spray them with chemicals, without realising that the majority of what we call 'weeds' can actually be eaten—either raw or steamed—and have excellent nutritional properties.

And on the larger scale, the picture I'd gleaned of the industrial food system was quite clear: the mass production of food, the massive amounts of pesticides, the vast quantities of fertilizer applied to the soil, its consequent exhaustion, the depletion of water resources ... The result of the industrial food system is food so poor in quality that it really can't come as a surprise that so many people nowadays have chronic diseases. Drinking, smoking, unhealthy food, emotional imbalance, stress, toxic air, polluted cities... What's more, the 'I-identity' fills the mind with hideous thoughts, chi stagnates, the mind becomes corrupted, the spirit rots... And still people are surprised when they hear the dreaded news: 'We've found a lump—it's cancer.'

OK... enough: back to the positive side.

I was spending three months on a permaculture farm in France with people who were very pleasant, although they were a little dogmatic in their thinking.

'In 2014 there will be total collapse, because oil production will reach its peak and there just won't be enough of it to keep the economic system going,' they told me.

'You really think it's going to happen that fast?'

They're frowning at me, and I can hear them thinking: 'How stupid can you get?'

It's pretty clear that I shouldn't try to mess with the image these people have of the world. The 'I-identity' loves to use the 'I'm saving the world' idea to keep itself going, and these ideas can keep us beautifully trapped in our mental prisons.

Permaculture and biodynamic farming are very interesting alternatives to the industrial food system. They produce healthy food without toxins and they don't require a lot of resources. Unfortunately, most permaculture courses charge those attending outrageous fees. Even permaculture has been turned into a business: a clear example of how the positive interest-based money system has hijacked even the sustainability movement.

The life of Masanobu Fukuoka provides a remarkable example of truly sustainable living. In his books, he discusses the fact that, for all our ability to reason and our scientific methods, our minds are too limited to truly comprehend nature and the world. Fukuoka came to this realisation only after himself having gone through intense suffering and a radical collapse of the 'I-identity'.

12. Feeding aidsbabies with sugar

Huge clouds of dust shoot up into the air as the black Mercedes speeds away on a little sand road in a slum outside of Cape Town. After the permaculture farm, I was staying with friends in South Africa: swimming, walking, visiting nature reserves. After a while, keen to observe the contrasts for which the country is so well-known, I ventured out into the slums.

'Tim, Tim! It's so good that you're here again!' And immediately I am embraced by the kind of friendly black woman so typical of South Africa.

'Good to see you too, Mrs Mgaba!'

'Did you see it, Tim?' she asks me. 'The Mercedes left another baby on our doorstep.'

'Seriously—again?'

I walk to the gate and see a black baby lying on the floor. The terrain of the orphanage is quite extensive, and includes a yard where fifty black kids and toddlers are playing. Mrs Mgaba runs the place and it gives her more than a few problems.

'What's up, Mrs Mgaba?' I say, when she comes up to me later in the day. 'I'm busy here, as you can see!'

Three little kids have scrambled on to my back.

'Do you know anything about medicine, Tim?' Mrs

Mgaba asks me.

'Not really that much,' I say. 'What's up? Are you OK?'

'Well, my legs hurt so much, and as for my eyes... I can barely see a thing.'

'Let's sit down for a bit.'

I carefully lower the kids to the ground and they run off into the dust.

I press on Mrs Mgaba's leg and ask her: 'Can you feel that?'

'No, not really,' she says, with a frown.

'Let me take a look at your eyes.'

She asks me what I think is the matter.

'I don't know much about medicine, but I do know that, when your eyes are discoloured and you can't feel your limbs properly, you probably have diabetes. And it looks to me like you have it quite badly.'

'Diabetes,' she says apprehensively. 'What's that?'

'Well,' I say, 'it's when your body is no longer able to regulate your blood sugar level.'

'And so what do I do?'

'Well, I would go the doctor.'

'But I don't have the money for that!' she cries.

'Okay, we could also take a look at your eating habits. What do you mainly eat?'

'Uhmmm, we start with sugar in the morning, in the afternoon we have Coca-Cola with sweet soup, and then rice and sugar in the evening.'

I can barely hold back my tears—what an absolute hell this is. Apart from the fact that most of the babies who are left at the orphanage are infected with HIV, all of them— babies and women alike—feed mainly on sugar, and it's completely destroying their health.

But the craziest thing of all is that some people in the slum are injecting themselves with HIV—yes, themselves, even their children in rare cases—so that they become HIV-positive and can get money from the government. Infect your baby with HIV, collect government funds for the baby, and drop the baby off at the orphanage—hardcore.

'Feeding aidsbabies with sugar... people injecting themselves with HIV-contaminated blood,' I think while lying in my warm bed. For the first time in ages my thoughts are beginning to get a little sticky. Slowly the thoughts fade away, but the extremes of the cancerous economic system which arises from our need to be 'someone' have once again been made pretty clear.

A small garden had been created in the orphanage with the help of permaculture techniques, but it was evident that this wasn't going to address the core of the problem. Due to the huge difference between rich and poor, South Africa is an extremely polarised society. Since the end of apartheid, capitalism has gone crazy, and a large proportion of the population is trapped in slums and in an aids/sugar/violence spiral where the level of suffering is incomprehensible to the average westerner.

We look back at the middle ages as an age of barbarity, but imagine what people in a couple of hundred years' time will say about our own era. Will they say: 'The 21st century was the time when humanity started to realise that having more does not mean being more'? Or will they say: 'This era was one of the darkest chapters in human history. In order to produce more material goods, in order—we thought—to alleviate our inner pain, we almost managed to destroy the planet.' Almost everybody during this epoch, it will seem, was mesmerized by fear and haunted by insatiable desires.

Our growth-based economic system originates in our craving to 'be more' and to 'have more', and those needs arise from the individual 'I'-identity' that needs to be distracted all the time with endless activities, and the quest for more and more material goods and permanent happiness. When there is an economic crisis, for example, people get scared because they're afraid of not having enough distractions for their 'I-identities'. No distractions often means being confronted with more pain, the pain, in fact, of being trapped in an 'I-identity' that is never truly at peace. As a consequence, war often breaks out after an economic crisis. As Yoda said: fear leads to anger leads to hate leads to suffering.

This whole social, cultural, psychological and economic edifice has been erected to avoid any confrontation with the void inside, the feeling of not being 'someone'. All perceived problems have their origin in the fear of being 'nobody'. All human madness arises from the identification with the thought-based 'I-identity', which is why the 'I-identity' or ego is often called the 'deluded mind', or the 'false mind', or 'the devil'. Moreover, the basic fact that humans are trapped in a deluded separate sense of self has been known for at least five thousand years, probably longer. The first descriptions of this separation—and ways to remedy it—can be found in Indian, Tibetan and Chinese scriptures and, in fact, in spiritual traditions all over the world.

On the plane back from South Africa I'm sitting next to a woman of considerable size.

'Oh my god,' she says in a high squeaky voice, 'these seats are so small, and as for the leg space...! And the air's so dry... This airline's terrible!'

'Hardcore suffering—ooh, poor you!' I answer sarcastically. 'We're having to cross a whole continent in a plane, and it's going to take you eight whole hours to get home from holiday!'

It's as if she hasn't heard me.

'The food in this plane is disgusting!'

I look her right in the face: 'Just shut up!'

'I'm calling the stewardess!' she says, indignantly.

'Fine, go right ahead. But before you do, I'd first like you to listen to a story I want to tell you.'

After a moment's pause, 'All right, go ahead,' she says. She clearly doesn't relish the idea of a confrontation in mid-air.

I turn to face her.

'An acquaintance of a friend in South Africa told me this a couple of weeks ago. It's a true story, and I think it's going to change your mind about how "uncomfortable" this airplane really is.

'Her parents were giving a party in a wealthy neighbourhood in Cape Town. At the end of the party three men with machine guns stormed the house and tied her parents to chairs. The men demanded money, and her father pointed them towards the location of the safe. There were around $2,000 dollars in the safe, but the burglars had found out from the cleaning lady, whom they'd also been threatening, that there was a second safe.

'The owner insisted that there was no other safe in the house, and the next thing he knew, the men had thrown his wife to the ground, spread her legs and were threatening to rape her unless he told them where the second safe was.

'The man succumbed to the pressure. He showed them the second safe and the burglars found around $200,000 inside, a huge amount in South Africa.

'And even though they had found this enormous amount of money, the youngest burglar still started raping the woman in front of her husband. After five minutes, he ejaculated, got up off her and casually said: "By the way, I've got AIDs."

'The woman was found to be HIV-positive, and six months later she killed herself.'

'Oh my god!'

The woman looks at me in total shock.

'So perhaps you'll understand now why I asked you to shut up.'

When I arrive at the airport I read in a newspaper that, for the first time since statistics began, there has been a day without murder in New York. Another article is talking about renewed 'humanitarian bombardments' in Iraq. Humanity can put a spacecraft on the moon—we call that progress—but we do not even teach our children how to balance emotions and be at peace. I mean, seriously—what a circus! Who could make it up?

If you want to understand human behaviour and where

all this madness is coming from, your questions can only be answered—or more precisely, dissolved—in the overcoming of the boundaries of the 'I-identity'.

Imagine being the Buddha, somehow reborn in this era, and finding millions of garden gnomes in your image all over the world. That must be the weirdest thing. Similarly, Jesus seems to have been a man of foresight, but I don't suppose he expected that people claiming to follow his teachings would launch massive wars, that priests would turn into child molesters or that cardinals would start dressing up like Santa Claus. Imagine Jesus finding out that the day of his birth has been turned into the biggest commercial consumption binge the world has ever seen. What a joke! Such examples of ignorance and misinterpretation can be seen in all societies, religions and spiritual traditions. The *true* meaning, for example, of the Islamic term 'jihad' has nothing to do with fighting with infidels or with other religions: it refers to the fight with the 'I-identity'.

If people could show real focus, on the other hand, then there would be genuine results, instead of child-molesting priests and backyards full of 'Buddha' gnomes. Change, however, is not a simple matter. Marcus Aurelius, the Roman emperor/philosopher, obviously knew that the Roman economy based on slave labour was barbaric, but did he try to change it? No. He played out his role, realising that certain changes—such as the Roman system of slavery (or, in our own era, the economic system)—take time, and that patterns have to play themselves out.

The attempt to turn yourself into a messiah who's going to change the world (so that, of course, you can be 'someone') is highly counterproductive, to put it mildly. For any sense of control is fundamentally illusory. If the 'I' is simply a thought, who actually is it who's making the decisions?

Let's repeat that: if the 'I' is simply a thought, who actually is it who's making the decisions?

Close your eyes and ask yourself: 'Who is in control?' The answer that will pop up is 'I'm in control' or, quite simply, 'me'. But if you can observe the thought 'I'm in control' or 'me', who is watching or controlling these thoughts? Obviously not the 'I' or the 'me'. And if the 'I' is not in control, does free will even exist?

All this can be figured out, by being honest, focused and alone. Think about this—ponder over it. At the beginning it's not easy.

13. Beer, fries, porn & pills

Back in the Netherlands, there was a time when I did nothing. Sometimes an old friend would call.

'Hey, Tim, how are you?'

'Yeah, perfect! You?'

'Well, you know, tired, working like hell... Suffering like we all are.'

'Not anymore,' I reply, 'but I know what you mean.'

'So what are you up to these days, Tim?'

'Not a lot, actually. What are you doing yourself?'

'Working in an office mostly. On Sundays, though, after a week of hard work, we buy a crate of beer and the biggest bag of fries in Amsterdam, watch some porn and sometimes take some pills. Feel like dropping by?'

'Yes, well... never mind... I'm good.'

Somehow, a couple of weeks later, I did end up at this guy's apartment. There were some internet videos playing. The first depicted a Japanese girl who was stuffing her vagina with live fish... interesting. The second video was something insane called *One man, one jar*. A naked man was slowly pushing a glass jar into his anus and, once the jar was almost entirely inside his ass, it accidently cracked and the man spent the remainder of the video pulling out blood-covered pieces of broken glass. Sick.

It was quite clear that the time had come for me to move on to a remote place, somewhere in nature, somewhere far away from this madness and a society where most people live through the same destructive patterns, day in day out.

Coincidentally, my good friend Michael had arrived at exactly the same point.

14. Forest gardening

A warm wind is blowing from the south and the hammock is swinging gently in the breeze. I roll from right to left and look out over a beautiful green valley, snow-covered mountains in the distance.

As I close my eyes, I start to dream about all the beautiful things there could be on this planet (a dream within a dream): luscious gardens filled with fresh produce, a sustainable economic system, a humanity that is sexually balanced through Taoist techniques, a culture which genuinely encourages self-enquiry instead of mocking it.

I drift off into further dreams, until I'm suddenly awoken by the honking of geese standing next to the hammock.

A year ago, I had decided to buy a house with my friend Michael so that we could have a quiet place to enjoy nature and build a forest garden using permaculture techniques.

The concept of a forest garden—which has been elaborately developed by the Englishman Martin Crawford—is an interesting one. A forest garden is a young forest which consists of seven 'layers': a top 'layer' consisting largely of nitrogen-fixing trees like Italian alders, a 'layer' of fruit and nut trees, a 'layer' of shrubs, a 'layer' of large herbaceous perennials, a 'layer' of small herbaceous perennials, climbers and root crops.

All the plants are edible or provide some kind of nutritional yield: seeds, nuts, fruits, berries, leaves, flowers, etc.

We're talking here about perennials (such as rhubarb) and so, with little work, except for the original planting, you can harvest year after year. In contrast, annuals—such as lettuce, cucumber, tomatoes, etc—have to be planted out every year, after tilling the soil and adding a lot of manure or compost.

It's a brilliant idea: in imitation of a young forest, a forest garden is perennial, requires little maintenance, provides high nutritional yield and is aesthetically pleasing.

So yes: there are some pretty good ideas out there to deal with some of the problems a lot of people perceive. However, these are all distractions from the primary issue, the one which has to be addressed before all others: finding out who you are, and finding out if reality is really as real as we think it is.

15. The difference between the 'being' state and enlightenment

Walking in a state of total relaxation I am exploring the forest near our house. Deer sprint away over small rivers, while sweet chestnuts cover the forest floor. Spanish cows with bells are grazing in the fields, and the sound of streams mixes with the chirping of the birds.

After eating a salad fresh from the garden, I sit in a chair and, for the first time in a while, open a book. I don't really read anymore with the aim of finding things out, but sometimes it can be a pleasure to appreciate the words of a sharp, focused mind.

I stop at a particular sentence and read it a couple of times, before it starts sinking in:

'Now, consciousness has identified with a form. Later, it understands that it is not that form and goes further. In a few cases it may reach the space, and very often, there it stops. In a very few cases, it reaches its real source, beyond all conditioning'—Sri Nisargadatta Maharaj.

Although I had already spent time many years ago thinking a lot about all this, emptying the mind of all mental formations, nevertheless, an itch had started up. The pressure had definitely started building again, although it took a while for me to be honest with myself about what I was observing. And I only really understood what it was when I read this sentence—over and over again, each time becoming clearer.

We're now coming to the more intense part of the book, so let's concentrate.

'Can it really be,' I thought, 'that there is further to go, that I've fooled myself again, that the "I-identity" has pulled another trick out of the hat?'

In one sense it didn't matter what happened, all was good, but a period of critical self-observation led me to realise that there was definitely still 'I-identification' with consciousness, and especially with the 'being' state, the feeling of recognising myself (as nothing) in everything.

The Zen Master Bassui describes this last trap in the following words: 'If you separate from all forms in your mind, and do not fall into the pit of formlessness, liberation will manifest. Destroy the world when it appears, and the void when it appears.'

Somehow, without being aware of it, I had become stuck in the 'being' state—'the pit of formlessness'. Until now.

The realisation of the 'being' state is a very powerful one, and abiding in the 'being' state seems to be the end of seeking. As a consequence, some people even become spiritual teachers. However, this is not the moment to stop investigating the source of consciousness.

How do you move beyond the 'being' state? Well, the first thing to do is to recognize that the 'I-identity' has subtly attached itself to the 'being' state. In my case, this recognition took many years to arrive.

Earlier, in chapter 10, I talked about 'side-effects', and these are typical of the 'being' state, since it is not really enlightenment. The 'being' state—the state of recognising yourself (as nothing) in everything—is the final trick of the 'I-identity', and I had remained trapped in it for years. (It's easy for things to get over-complicated when using language: the abiding state of recognising yourself (as nothing) in everything is therefore simply referred to here as the 'being' state.)

You might be thinking now that all of this seems so difficult. And it is. Even though enlightenment is the simplest thing there is, piercing through the layers of delusion to come to realisation is the hardest thing there is. This process is no 'walk in the park' where—whoosh!—enlightenment suddenly just happens. Any awakening along 'walk in the park' lines is not enlightenment at all but rather a realisation of the 'being' state. Piercing through the layers of delusion takes years of dedication.

The main reason for the writing of this book is that almost nobody (except, for example, some recommended authors mentioned later on) is aware of this. This is why the spiritual swamp is so vast, and why teachers are so eager to share with the world their ideas about 'being everything, being nothing'.

You will notice that, from here on in, the approach of this book changes from the narrative to the explanatory. Why? Because from this moment on we will be exploring topics, true understanding of which can only derive from direct experience.

Obviously, what is said in this chapter cannot be understood intellectually: only through hammering at your 'I-identity', in solitude, will progress be made. The reason for trying to describe the difference between the 'being' state and enlightenment (both of which are actually indescribable) is to enable anyone who embarks on the real struggle with the 'I-identity' to recognise the trap of the 'being' state when it presents itself.

First of all, let's clarify some terms, starting with experience.

An experience consists of sensory input that is filtered through the perceptual centres. Experiences can be classified as physical, mental, energetic or spiritual. The physical comprises all bodily sensations, the mental all thought-based activity, and this is really all that's consciously experienced by most people nowadays. By energetic we mean the experiences related to chi; everything is energy or chi but, once you develop the necessary sensitivity, it is easier to feel it in living things, such as the channels of the body, plants and animals. The spiritual includes out-of-body experiences, experiences of oneness, blissful states and other subtle 'bodies' which have been described in detail in various esoteric traditions.

However, all these things are experienced by an 'I-identity'—there is a 'someone' who is experiencing these different states. Therefore all experience is subjective, and there can never be an objective experience or objective knowledge. And we can never be one hundred percent certain that any subjective experience is really true, which is why the struggle for enlightenment is the search for an absolute truth—the absolute.

Here are some brief definitions of other important terms, which I will then go on to elucidate further.

- *The 'being' state*: The state of recognising yourself (as nothing) in everything, also called presence, spaciousness, oneness, space, void, I-am-ness, the state of 'I am', universal consciousness, atman, beingness, emptiness, stillness, etc. Most spiritual teachers mistake this state for enlightenment.

- *Enlightenment*: Surrender to the absolute. Also called nirvana, Buddhahood, self-realisation, awakening, bodhi, moksha, truth-realisation, deveikut, illumination, satchitananda, sahaja samadhi, etc. On an energetic level, enlightenment happens when the heart-knot is permanently dissolved (for further details, see chapter 17).

- *The absolute*: That which is beyond all consciousness and which includes all consciousness. Also called Brahman, God/Father, Shiva, Wu Chi, One Mind, Truth, Infinity, Awareness, Ultimate Reality, Source, Tao, Ein-Sof, Allah, Dharmakaya, True Mind, Buddha-nature, etc. Many people use these terms to refer to the 'being' state but, properly used, they always refer to the absolute.

The 'being' state

When somebody, an 'I', looks, for example, at a tree, that 'I' thinks and feels that the tree is separate from him or her, that there *is* an 'I' looking at the tree; a separation between the 'I' that looks and the 'tree' that is being looked at. The 'tree' and the 'I' are nevertheless both in your mind. The world you see is not absolutely real: it is a projection created in your mind.

Once you let go of all mental interpretations—beliefs, concepts, words, thoughts, ideas, etc—there will come a moment where the idea 'tree' disappears, and the idea 'I' as well. The 'I' (consciousness) consequently recognises itself in the 'tree' (consciousness), because the 'tree' and the 'I' are not really separate from each other—they are one, both are consciousness. There is no 'I' that looks at the tree anymore—there is only consciousness. A state of mind ensues in which you recognise yourself, as consciousness, in everything—the 'being' state, often described as an intense sense of being, presence or emptiness. Since the 'being' state is not just a temporary occurrence, but an abiding state, it is commonly mistaken for enlightenment.

This is the state I'd been in after what happened in Nicaragua.

However, even though the 'being' state is an amazing one, it is still an experience, and is not enlightenment. The 'being' state—realising all is consciousness or an intense abiding sense of presence or emptiness—is still being experienced by a subtle 'I-identity', so this is not the end of seeking. A 'still' mind is not an enlightened mind.

This misconception is commonplace: people believe that enlightenment is the ability to be in the 'now' all the time, in the 'being' state all the time, or to recognise yourself (as consciousness) in everything all the time. People mistake enlightenment for the void, emptiness, when the mind is blank or there is nothing there, and don't realise that one has to go through these states to reach the absolute. (In Buddhism, this is described as moving through the eight jhanas, of which the last four are formless states: infinite space, infinite consciousness, nothingness, neither perception nor non-perception.)

Let's emphasize that abiding in the 'being' state is already pretty amazing, and there is clearly nothing wrong with that. However, the fact that people mistake it for enlightenment, and start teaching this (often for money), is disturbing. It means that the chances of encountering teachings and teachers that lead to true liberation become increasingly rare. The larger the spiritual swamp, the harder it becomes to find a way out.

True self-enquiry has nothing to do with changing your state of being—it is about finding out who or what is experiencing all these states in the first place.

And how do the Zen terms of *satori* and *kensho* relate to this? These terms (which are generally found in Rinzai although not Soto Zen) are actually interchangeable and usually refer to temporary spiritual epiphanies. Zen masters describe kensho—which takes considerable effort to attain—as being deep or shallow, thereby clearly showing that kensho is an experience, not a final realisation. Some real Zen masters make it clear that kensho is just the beginning of real spiritual training, after which apprentices still need many years of deep meditation if they are to have a chance of attaining true enlightenment.

Throughout the course of history, it seems that a fair number of Zen masters have become enlightened. True Zen training remains a valid path, although these days it is very hard to find a true Zen master.

True Zen masters as well warn about the 'being' state. Zen Master Bassui describes the 'being' state like this: 'The mind suddenly becomes clear, the division between inner and outer no longer exists, everything dissolves perfectly. If you take these perceptions to be real, it is like seeing a fish's eye as a pearl. When this perceived world manifests, investigate thoroughly right where you are. What is it that is investigating?'

Master Hsu Yun (Xu Yun), a legendary Ch'an master,

describes how, after the initial opening of the mind, a further period of meditation is required to wipe out remaining psychological habits and reach true enlightenment. The Korean Son Master Chinul states that, after an initial understanding/awakening, cultivation has to continue, until it matures into the ultimate awakening.

In the Kena Upanishad, it is stated quite clearly:

> 'The teacher says:
> If you think you know this well
> Then you know very little.
> What is known by you
> Is only the appearance of Brahman
> That strikes the senses.
> So continue with your studies,
> My dear sons and daughters.'

And so to move further on, one has to ask the questions: to what background does this 'being' state take place? Where does this 'being' state come from? Who is it that is feeling this amazing sense of being? Who is it that is recognising themselves in everything?

It looks now as if there are levels, but that is not the case: there are no levels, only more illusions. Most so-called spiritual teachers get stuck in this trap their whole lives without even realising it. Many nowadays believe that abiding in the 'being' state is enlightenment. Well, unfortunately, that's not the case.

Enlightenment

So what is enlightenment? The 'I-identity' (identification with mind and body) functions as a 'knot' between the absolute and the physical body. When enlightenment happens, this 'knot' is dissolved permanently, resulting in surrender to the absolute. The absolute can never be experienced directly yet, paradoxically, it is everything. When there is surrender to the absolute, there is no longer identification (emotional attachment) with any experience in consciousness, including the 'being' state.

The difference between the 'being' state and enlightenment

To clarify, think of a tree. Imagine sitting on a branch, not knowing you are in a tree. The physical is the sensation of touching the bark of the branch. The mental is the labelling of the branch with the thought 'branch'. The energetic is being aware of the flow of chi in the branch. The spiritual is realising for a short while that the branch is part of a whole tree (the unity experience of a tree). The 'being' state is the abiding experience that you and the tree are one—the experience of being a separate 'I-identity' has mostly fallen away. The absolute is the space in which the tree exists: it both is beyond the tree and includes the tree. It can never be experienced directly, yet it includes everything. Enlightenment is surrender to the absolute.

As another way of looking at it: a person ('I-identity') lives in the world, not knowing all is consciousness. The physical are the sensations that arise when the world is perceived: touch, smell, taste, etc. The mental is the labelling of the world with the thought 'world'. The energetic is being aware of the flow of chi in the world. The spiritual is realising for a short while that the world is in fact consciousness (the unity experience of consciousness). The 'being' state is the abiding experience of consciousness as a whole; the experience of being a separate 'I-identity' has mostly fallen away. The absolute is that which both is beyond consciousness and includes all consciousness. It can never be experienced directly, yet it includes everything. Enlightenment is surrender to the absolute.

In the 'being' state, there is still 'I-identification' with the abiding 'state of oneness': that is not the case with surrender to the absolute. Surrender to the absolute does not mean that you are knocked out, unconscious, beyond pain, permanently in total bliss. No—not at all. It is an abiding state of surrender in which, paradoxically, one still functions (eats, acts, breathes, shits, etc), but there is no longer any 'I-identification' whatsoever, and so there is no more suffering.

The process of awakening is the step by step dis-identification from all subjective experiences—physical, mental, energetic, spiritual, including dis-identification from both the 'I-identity' and from the 'being' state. So it is literally to break out of an illusion: the illusion that you are a separate 'I-identity', the illusion that you are the body and mind, the illusion that perceptual reality is absolutely real, and the illusion that any subjective experiences are absolutely true.

Many eastern spiritual/meditation systems (Taoism, many forms of Buddhism, Yoga, Kashmir Shaivism) have been seriously misunderstood by western spiritual/meditation teachers because a lot of western teachers are ignorant of subtle energetic states and spiritual experiences, and hence focus only on the mind. As a result of this ignorance, the experience of the flow of energy in the body, or of some different state of consciousness, is often assumed to be enlightenment itself. As a result, most people assume they have finished before they have even begun.

Some people, for example, relax their body and mind,

feel for the first time some intense energy or an incredible heat going up the spine, and mistakenly conclude that that is enlightenment. Others have an experience of spiritual unity or find themselves abiding in the 'being' state, and mistakenly believe they are enlightened. Some say that, when people sleep, they are in the enlightened state. This is totally untrue. During sleep, the mind ('I-identity') is active, but lost in dream states.

In most spiritual and meditation systems taught in the west or by westerners (especially in the non-duality, fake Zen and neo-Advaita scenes), it is often forgotten that a very important aspect of the struggle for enlightenment is not only mental dis-identification (the dissolution of the part of the 'I-identity' made up of thoughts and emotions), but also energetic and spiritual dis-identification (the dissolution of the part of the 'I-identity' that is linked to the energetic and spiritual bodies, called 'sheaths' in eastern traditions). This process releases tremendous energy, and it is this energy which, after considerable effort in meditation, dissolves/resolves the 'I-identity', resulting in surrender to the absolute. (For further details on this process, see chapter 17.)

Nisargadatta Maharaj makes a clear distinction between consciousness (which in the pure form is the 'being' state and which he refers to as universal consciousness) and awareness (Brahman). The Zen Master Tozan describes the difference between the 'being' state and enlightenment in some detail, and his work is nowadays referred to as 'the five degrees of Zen Master Tozan'. Ramana Maharshi also clearly explains the difference between Kevala Nirvikalpa Samadhi (when the heart-knot opens, but closes again) and Sahaja Nirvikalpa Samadhi (enlightenment, when the heart-knot is permanently dissolved) (see, for example, *Sri Ramana Gita*). In essence, in Kevala Samadhi, the mind ('I-identity') is active, but sunk in light; in Sahaja Samadhi, the mind ('I-identity') is 'dead', resolved in the Self. (Ramana Maharshi's Sahaja Samadhi is, in fact, the same as Gautama Buddha's Nirvana.) Most western teachers who quote Ramana Maharshi totally ignore this very important esoteric/energetic point concerning the heart-knot.

If you investigate deeply into spiritual and esoteric traditions, you will realise that what is being said in this book is the same as what you will find in any real spiritual tradition that aims at full awakening. Most people in the non-duality and neo-Advaita scenes, however, only scratch the surface and are unaware of the energetic/esoteric aspects of enlightenment. As a result, most 'teachers' mistakenly assume the 'being' state to be enlightenment.

After enlightenment?

Well... with enough honesty and persistence, anyone can find that out. But to provide a simple illustration, using again the example of the tree: after enlightenment you're still sitting on the branch, but there is the realisation that the whole tree (consciousness) is space (the absolute). Sounds complicated, but it's not: it's so simple that it is literally beyond imagination. One still lives in the world as a human being, but there is an abiding state of surrender since nothing was, is or will ever be wrong. An awakened person is calm, unworried, tranquil, balanced, content, humble and peaceful. After enlightenment, no longer is energy wasted on destructive egocentric activities. Life flows, like a fish and a river flowing together.

Who becomes enlightened? In the western non-duality and Advaita scenes, you often hear that 'nobody' becomes enlightened, that reality is unreal. If you hear someone saying this, take a hammer, hit their hand, and see how 'nobody' is doing. Obviously, this 'nobody' talk is nonsense. True, reality is not absolutely real, but this does not mean it is not relatively real to a person living in their respective relative reality. Absolute reality manifests as relative reality—they are in essence one.

Clearly, the 'I-identity' (the identification with mind and body) has to fall away for enlightenment to occur, but the body does not die—the 'I-identification' dies and is replaced by the realisation of the absolute, the Self, Buddha-nature, etc.

Let's clarify. First, someone is trapped in the 'I-identity'. Next, they realise that the 'I-identity' is a mental prison, and a tough struggle begins to dissolve the 'I-identity'. After that, the 'I-identity' falls away—mostly—and the 'being' state ensues. And in the end, the 'I-identity' surrenders to the absolute: enlightenment occurs.

To an observer, a sage may seem to act as 'someone' again, but this is simply due to the illusion of separation believed by the 'I-identity' of the observer. To the sage him- or herself, there is no longer identification with a separate 'I-identity'. But to the 'outside world', to those who have no true understanding of this, the absolute now 'manifests' itself through the body and mind of the sage; clearly, it does not manifest through 'nobody'. It can only be described in terms of paradox.

Words create paradoxes, agreed. Describing the indescribable in words creates paradoxes, agreed. Wasting time trying to understand enlightenment intellectually is a common distraction employed by the 'I-identity', but it's like trying to understand what being drunk is like when you've never had a drop of alcohol. Get hammered, then you know what being drunk is like. Hammer down the 'I-identity', and one day all paradoxes are gone.

16. The stay-trapped approach versus the take-action approach

Effective teachers/teachings and useful books about self-enquiry focus on the recommendation that one should take honest, concentrated action in solitude: the take-action approach. These are rare. Ineffective teachers/teachings simply give extensive descriptions of the end-result of self-enquiry or the nature of reality and experience: the approach they advocate can be described as the stay-trapped approach. These are plentiful.

The take-action approach is prescribed by teachers or writers who have surrendered to the absolute. The stay-trapped approach is adopted by teachers or writers who are in the 'being' state, or in some other state of consciousness altogether.

Let's take a simple look at the difference between these two approaches. Teachers using the take-action approach say: 'Discover it for yourself—whatever the price.' Teachers using the stay-trapped approach say things like: 'Enlightenment is oneness... consciousness is all... there is only the now... just allow everything... rest in awareness... you are already totally complete... effort is useless... just be the intimacy and sensitivity that underlies reality.'

The take-action approach is about taking action yourself, alone with iron determination. The stay-trapped approach is about listening to 'teachers' express and explain their views and experiences of 'that which cannot be known'.

The take-action approach can lead to results, in the sense that people might actually embark, alone, on a process of true self-enquiry, which may one day culminate in a surrender to the absolute. The stay-trapped approach leads people to become stuck in the spiritual swamp.

Some might say that I am being too judgmental here. However, a distinction needs to be drawn between judging in the sense of simply observing, and judging.

Spirituality should not be an excuse to stop exercising your critical faculties—on the contrary, true spirituality is about exercising the utmost critical discrimination, especially towards yourself. Without developing some real sense as to what actually might be useful on a path of self-enquiry, one can drown in the spiritual swamp for years, decades, even a lifetime.

The extent to which the stay-trapped approach has spread can be seen everywhere: at meetings, retreats, question-and-answers sessions, etc; whilst, owing to the huge increase in size of the spiritual swamp, the genuine take-action approach is becoming increasingly difficult to find. Consequently, fewer and fewer people seem to have the remotest idea as to what true self-enquiry really entails. Richard Rose puts it brilliantly when he states: 'The chances for making personal contacts for spiritual purposes are inversely proportional to the density and madness of the population.'

To make some sense of the spiritual swamp, we can, in short, observe the following. The majority of the human population is identified with and emotionally attached to language (in other words, thoughts, and especially the thought 'I') and form (the body and perceptions/feelings), which together form the 'I-identity'.

Some people move beyond form conceptually, but not experientially. For example, there are scientists who know through scientific theory that the universe is in essence one, but they do not directly experience the universe as one.

Other people have experiences of unity through meditation, drugs, breathing, yoga, etc; these are non-abiding (temporary) experiences of god-consciousness, unity-consciousness, etc. Some even reach the 'being' state, the abiding experience that all is one; one can see oneself in everything, beyond words, beyond form, such that dualities such as right and wrong no longer apply. Some surrender to the absolute.

Let's emphasize that there is nothing wrong with teaching people about meditation, mindfulness, energy and other techniques which enable them to feel better and more at ease. This is all fantastic, and people who teach these things provide a valuable service for their fellows. However, there are a lot spiritual teachers who talk about liberation and enlightenment, while what they are actually doing is, in essence, selling—for money—a commercialised stay-trapped approach.

Most people are not interested in true self-enquiry, and there is nothing wrong with that at all. But for those who are, it is important to know how to navigate the spiritual swamp.

True liberation *is* possible, and any practice which does not have this as its end result is useless (unless the goal is not enlightenment, in which case there are many useful practices and techniques for becoming calm and relaxed). An effective teacher has surrendered to the absolute. An ineffective teacher is often in a non-abiding state or in the abiding 'being' state. So how can you recognize the difference?

Some effective teachers remain anonymous, some may

write a book or two, whilst there are also those who radiate such clarity, or talk in such a focused way, that they attract attention without even trying. Genuine Buddhist, Taoist or other masters guide their students for free. Ineffective teachers (and there are lots of ways to be an ineffective teacher) mostly sit in front of groups of people and speak or hold retreats and charge their audiences for the privilege. It could be said, in the words of Alan Watts: 'Spiritual pride is the desire to admire oneself as a supreme success in the art of love and unselfishness.'

Let's have a look at some of the tricks, traps, delusions, ambiguities and distortions that are prevalent in the spiritual swamp. Key aspects to watch for in the stay-trapped approach are as follows:

Group (question-and-answer) meetings: Most so-called teachers like to sit in front of a group of eager students. If such a teacher answers questions, the answers are often totally ineffective, because self-enquiry is not about answers—it's about finding out who is asking questions in the first place. People may leave such meetings 'enlightened', sure—in that they leave the lecture hall with a bit less money in their pockets!

If you look online, you can find some truly appalling question-and-answer sessions, consisting of the most unfocused of questions and the strangest and vaguest of answers, where the whole crowd of questioners is getting high on how 'in the moment' or 'realised' the master is. What's more, none of them ever asks any difficult or serious questions in the first place, and the majority of teachers of the stay-trapped approach simply avoid direct questions about tricky topics such as sex, the details of the process of enlightenment, the absolute and the 'being state'.

And if they are questioned about the charges they levy, they will probably give some vague reply about how money is used simply as an 'energy-exchange'.

A true master will always direct your attention back towards self-enquiry, or towards the process of the deconstruction of the 'I-identity'. A true master knows that no answer will ever satisfy the 'I-identity', but if necessary, pertinent answers can be given, for free, to questions like: 'How do you deal with sexual energy while you're in solitude?' 'If the absolute is the end of searching, who is it who is talking now?' 'Why have I been trapped in the same patterns for twenty years?' 'Why do so few actually wake up?' 'Why do I recognise myself in everything?'

It is crucial to stay away from groups, meetings and organisations in general, because a true process of awakening can only take place in solitude. An exception to this is a genuine Buddhist, Zen or Taoist monastery, although nowadays these are rare. Some do still exist in the east, but in the west you mostly find fake imitations.

There can, of course, be instances when an individual seeker goes to a true master (one who has surrendered to the absolute), and that master provides a short focused answer aimed at encouraging the student to take action himself. Such masters do not organise events or meetings on their own initiative. Why not? Because when there is surrender to the absolute, nothing can ever be wrong, so why change anything?

Money: Money and the 'I-identity' are so intertwined that people who charge for meetings or one-to-one sessions obviously have a second agenda, even if only a subtle one. Most spiritual teachers know nothing about the money system, so when they ask for money at group sessions, private appointments or retreats, they are unwittingly supporting a very destructive system. There is a very good reason for Jesus's strong opposition to the money lenders.

Now that the current economic system which relies on the creation of money with positive interest has been explained (see chapter 10), it should be clear how absurd it is in this context to ask for money.

'But what about the money I had to pay to buy this book!' you may ask. A valid point, but the price for the paper version has been deliberately kept as low as possible and simply covers production costs. Moreover, the electronic version is either free (for example, on www.beeraidsbabiesenlightenment.com or through Smashwords) or available as cheaply as the distributor allows (for example, through Amazon). Any money generated will be used to finance the distribution of free copies.

A true 'teacher' never asks for money, a donation or, indeed, anything else. This is an extremely important point, because the fact that the practice of charging money has become widespread clearly demonstrates how extensive the spiritual swamp has become. This simple fact—charging money—exposes a huge number of spiritual charlatans who advocate a stay-trapped approach. Whilst there is no guarantee that a spiritual teacher who does *not* ask for money is teaching an honest take-action approach, it is fair to say that the overwhelming majority of fake spiritual teachers charge for meetings and retreats. This makes it a lot easier to separate the wheat from the chaff: just look for those who are asking for money, and there you will also find strong attachment to the 'I-identity'.

You are already enlightened—do not seek—no effort is needed: It's absolutely amazing the way some teachers can sit in front of a group and say things like: 'Just allow yourself to be... You are already enlightened... No effort is required... Stop seeking'.

So I'm just supposed to give up, while still trapped in the same behavioural patterns and the illusion of the 'I-identity'? You can't get rid of your chains by just allowing them to be, or by pretending they're not there. Neither does painting them gold and charging people to come and look at them while you talk about how beautiful they are have any effect at all. Chains have to be broken: that is the only way.

There's a lot of this 'effortless' talk to be found in western non-duality and neo-Advaita circles. Obviously, it's easy enough to figure out that 'all is one' and, for many, to set up shop and start teaching (in return for money) 'effortless' non-duality seems nowadays to be the next logical step.

However, the realisation that all is one is just the beginning. Years of sustained effort are necessary to eradicate all the defilements of the 'I-identity', to discover the true essence of the 'I'.

There are many money-oriented spiritual movements which are essentially all talk and scarcely skim the surface of what is really required. They may say, for example, that meditation is entirely unnecessary—despite the fact that, for thousands of years across all serious spiritual traditions, the practice of intense meditation has proved indispensable.

This distortion can also be seen in yoga. Traditionally, this was a system of exercises designed to prepare and support the body for the efforts required to discover the true nature of the 'I'. In the west, yoga has been reduced to a series of simple physical stretches. Oneness universities, non-dual radio stations and podcasts, non-dual apps for your iPhone, Instagram gurus, facebook spirituality, thousands of Advaita and non-duality websites—the insanity in the spiritual swamp is both unbelievable and at the same time funny. The fact that people are trapped in their 'I-identity' is one thing, but that millions or even billions spend a large part of the day in their 'digital identity' is even stranger. No wonder some true masters prefer to keep their mouths shut and disappear into the mountains, or only share their teachings with that rare thing, the honest student.

On one level, it's true to say that the concept and the feeling of making an effort are also illusory, and that you never actually lost what you are looking for—but one can only come to that realisation after an intense effort has been made: not the other way around. People love reading the accounts of the moment when a certain master became enlightened, but often overlook the fact that this realisation could only happen after years of sustained effort and intense self-enquiry.

The claim that everyone is already enlightened (or possesses Buddha-nature, is one with the absolute, etc) and that, as a consequence, no effort is needed to realise this is simply ridiculous. It is like saying that a hardened criminal is essentially a good person, solely because his intrinsic nature is good. Whilst this could be said to be true at an ultimate level, on the conventional level a hardened criminal will only come to be seen as a good person if he or she goes through the extensive behavioural therapy and mental training which are prerequisites of genuine reform.

People have conjured up all sorts of nihilistic ideas, employing concepts of no-effort, emptiness, the void, no-mind, etc, in order to promote various insane versions of the stay-trapped approach. The claim that effort is not necessary because the 'I-identity' and all its defilements are part of the Buddha-nature simply promotes mental inertia. Tough, seemingly endless struggles, in the form of meditation or some other form of persistent self-enquiry, have always preceded true realisation.

In a nutshell, the recommendation of 'effortlessness' advocated by proponents of the stay-trapped approach is useless: convincing yourself that no effort is required, that all effort is illusory, will never lead to the collapse of the 'I-identity'. Those who teach 'effortlessness' are often trapped in the 'being' state: you will never hear this message from those who have surrendered to the absolute.

A glimpse: Perhaps, thanks to the presence of a teacher who is in the 'being' state, you will get a brief glimpse of it yourself. The 'I-identity', however, will quickly return. A glimpse or any temporary change in consciousness, even abiding in the 'being' state, can never be the end of seeking.

The spiritual family: Whilst solitude is an essential constituent of a genuine take-action approach, the vague 'spiritual process' so typical of the stay-trapped approach usually involves being part of some spiritual organisation or meditation group, all the while maintaining your job, family, friends, relationships, etc. A lengthy period of solitude is a crucial requirement for real progress, and it is on this issue that we see the main dividing-line between the overwhelming majority of people who practise 'spirituality' as a hobby, and the few honest ones who are willing to pay the ultimate price by literally deconstructing their 'I-identity' on their own.

Just a decision—'speed' courses: There are 'speed courses' offered nowadays which claim, for example, that in two days you can take the decision to be enlightened. Even the Buddha struggled six years, in solitude, to achieve enlightenment. True masters from India, Tibet, Kashmir, China, Japan, Vietnam, Korea, the Middle East, etc, have all known for centuries if not millennia that the realisation of enlightenment is far from being a 'walk in the park' or the result of a speed course, but rather is a process that takes many years. We in the west, of course, know better! Here it's all about commercialisation, and we wrap it all up for a quick sale. So fortunate westerners can pay through the nose for a couple of days or a long weekend retreat, perhaps a couple of weeks, and buy 'enlightenment'. I think it should be clear by now how totally absurd such a concept is.

We are all one: Breaking your way out of your mental prison (the 'I-identity') is not the same as pretending your prison is actually a five-star hotel. In other words, if you want to stay trapped, let's do nothing and pretend the prison is a nice club where we can hold lectures, meditate together, be together and pretend to be one.

Being in the moment: Since the end of the 20th century, certain spiritual teachers have become very famous by stating that one just has to be in 'the now' or in 'the actual moment'. Has true surrender to the absolute ever happened by trying to live permanently in 'the actual moment'? Of course not. The writers of books on 'the now' or 'the actual moment' may have had breakthroughs, but that was not because of trying to be in 'the now'. It happened after they had experienced years of depression and intense suffering. In short: an intense battle.

The Zen Master Bankei struggled so intensively for enlightenment that true surrender happened only when he was literally almost dead. Afterwards, he became very famous in Japan for his lectures in which he said that the only action anyone has to take to be at peace is to 'abide in the unborn'. The 'unborn' here means the absolute. So how many people actually managed to 'abide in the unborn', like Bankei, after hearing this? Probably none. Why not? Because Bankei had omitted the most important point: that true surrender can only happen after hard struggle. He said that his own struggles had been unnecessary and had only happened because there had been no good teacher around to show him the way. But it's not about being shown the way: true surrender can only happen after intense effort.

Bankei was right in saying that 'abiding in the unborn' is our original One Mind, of course, but this realisation cannot be understood by the 'I-identity'. The 'I-identity' and its ideas are like stains on a perfect mirror. And yes, the idea of achieving or struggling for enlightenment is also a stain, but stains do not remove themselves.

Being a popular teacher does not automatically mean being an effective teacher. Obviously, 'I-identities' love the 'just be in the now' kind of talk, because it basically means that everything can stay the same and no effort is required. If these popular teachings were actually effective, where are the millions of people who have ended their search?

Listening to the same teachings over and over again: A lot of seekers keep coming back to listen to the same teachings over and over again. The fact that they have to do that just goes to show how ineffective such teachings are.

Smooth talk: If you look through the healing, spiritual, philosophical, esoteric, transcendental, non-dual and psychology sections of bookstores, not to speak of the many websites on these subjects, almost all feature beautiful words like love, emptiness, presence, being, now, awareness, awake, light, silence. Some so-called gurus are so 'at one' with everything that they seem to have lost all common sense; or else they use such vague and glib terminology in their books, retreats and meetings that you begin to wonder if they're high on drugs.

Some of the most focused spiritual teachers of the 20th century, for example Richard Rose or Sri Nisargadatta Maharaj, were notorious for being very direct, and sometimes addressing individual students in a way that was almost aggressive. Why? These men had surrendered to the absolute and knew what a battle the true 'I-enquiry' really is. One could say that, through their directness, they were trying to administer to the 'I-identity' a form of shock treatment.

There is no perceiver: 'There is no perceiver... Everything just happens... You are already there... Life without a centre... Just be' are statements which are often heard. Just picture it: 'Honey, I'm home from the non-dual meeting! And guess what? I'm not the perceiver!' Imagine the wife's reaction: 'Okay darling, that's great. Here's a beer—now go and sit on the couch and calm down.'

Food: Eating healthy nutritious food is a great idea. Improving your health and energy levels by improving your diet is well worth it. However, nowadays people link certain foods to a feeling of 'greater spiritual attunement', which is nonsense. You might feel better on a healthy diet, but that has nothing to do with spirituality. Spirituality is about finding out who is feeling—or eating—in the first place. Someone can spend their whole life focusing on living as long and as healthily as possible, without ever taking the next step: 'Who is living this life in the first place?'

Talking or reading about awakened beings and their qualities: We can talk about what an awakened being might be like (integrated, honest, at one, peaceful, taking action through non-action, etc), but listening to or reading such words is not going to lead to the manifestation of these qualities.

Going wild: Self-enquiry may release strong inner energies which you never knew existed. Don't let these energies take control, don't let these energies make you go wild. If things get totally out of control energetically, educate yourself in energy techniques to restore some balance. But don't let these techniques distract you. Use any increase in energy that arises to intensify your focus.

Parties: Non-dual parties, which you have to attend as 'no one'... because all are one... But everyone has to pay for a separate ticket, of course. Gotta love the money system!

The happiness of the 'I-identity': Conversations about happiness usually go something like this: 'Oh, I'm so unhappy. What can I do?' Well, simply get the 'someone' who feels the happiness and unhappiness out of the way, and you will be beyond happiness and unhappiness. 'So will that make me happy?'

Light: Even if your whole body feels clear and light, you still need to ask yourself: 'Who is feeling all this clarity?'

Attention: One often hears it said that 'where attention goes, energy flows'. But even attention requires a subtle effort. Ask yourself, 'Who is it who is putting in the attention?'

Pride: 'I know it all—I am a sage—I have finished—I am enlightened—I have surrendered to the absolute.' If you find yourself thinking like this, even at a very subtle level, you have become trapped in the swamp of pride. In order to pull yourself out of the swamp, just ask yourself: 'Who is thinking this? Who is it who feels they've finished?' In the enlightened state, there is no self-definition of any kind.

Even a minuscule amount of pride has a 'stench of enlightenment' to it. In *The Three Pillars of Zen* it is stated: 'Enlightenment, while revealing our solidarity with all things (thus bringing into accurate focus our distorted inner vision), paradoxically gives rise to a fine mist of pride in such an accomplishment, and this masks the inherent purity of the One Mind. So long as this defilement remains there is lingering disquiet.' Zen masters say that it can take months to get rid of the most obvious stench of enlightenment, two to three years to get rid of a more subtle stench, and even longer to get rid of the most subtle and thus most insidious stench.

No-mind, nothingness, oneness, emptiness, it's all conscious-ness: Entertaining spiritual concepts such as these—or even experiencing reality in such a way—cannot bring one closer to the absolute. An experience of emptiness, or when the mind goes blank, a great feeling of tranquillity and quiet-ness arises, when you recognise yourself as 'nothing' in everything—these have nothing to do with enlightenment. The absolute is beyond even emptiness, so lingering on these terms or attempting to 'abide in the void' is simply another distraction.

Also, you often hear many modern teachers saying that there is no mind, that they have no mind. This is absurd as well. The meaning of 'no-mind' is not that there is no mind—it means that after realisation the absolute and the mind are seen to be the same.

Son Master Chinul warns that a practice of no-think-ing (or excessive focus on emptiness) can lead to aloofness, feelings of superiority, arrogance, indifference or a nihilistic attitude. It often results in someone claiming to be enlight-ened while exhibiting the kind of clearly 'unenlightened' behaviour associated with defilements (also known as habit-energies, vasanas, desire-impulses, etc) that are still active. Keep digging deeper.

Martial arts: The practice of martial arts might make you feel stronger, more energetic and focused, but they have nothing to do with self-enquiry. There are physical disciplines—like judo and karate—and energetic disciplines—like aikido, kung fu and tai chi. But the real point of acquiring all that energy is to focus on the question: 'Who is fighting or defending him- or herself in the first place?' In fact, it could be said that, if we wish to have a peaceful world, step one would be to stop teaching people how to fight.

Books: There have been some amazing books and poems written in the east and the west. Books, poems or texts written, for example, by western transcendentalists (Emerson, Whitman, Thoreau, etc) or true masters (Hanshan, Hui-Neng, Huang Po, Chinul, Hsu Yun, Ikkyu, Ryokan, Hui Hai, Bassui, Dogen, etc) may generate tremendous insight, or even literally make you cry because of their focus, depth, simplicity, beauty, humour and sensitivity. They are all highly recommended. However, most of these can only really be valued, understood or appreciated once you have started struggling to find out who you really are—or once you are done with the struggle.

Other books with a philosophical or spiritual nature may be immensely popular or inspiring to read, but that does not automatically mean that these writings are therefore effective in encouraging true self-enquiry. Most 'spiritual' authors that publish one book after another, do so for one reason and one reason only: money. After all, a large number of expensive boks are simply not neccessary to convey a simple message. And in fact, the books and teachings on this subject that are *really* useful are rarely popular. Why not? Because they tell you that a true struggle takes a long time and total dedication; most people are not remotely willing to even begin considering such an effort.

It's all just a dream: Only someone who is still dreaming labels a dream as 'a dream'. Using the argument 'It's all just a dream' as a justification for doing whatever you want is obviously another version of the 'stay-trapped' approach.

Marriages/relationships: A process of awakening—and the piercing through all the layers of delusion and emotional attachment that this entails—cannot be undertaken whilst remaining married or in any intimate relationship.

Rebel: The 'I-identity' of the spiritual rebel is still an 'I-identity'.

Transmission: In Zen circles, you hear a lot about transmissions in the lineage of the Buddha. Anything transmissible is perceivable, so has nothing to do with the end of seeking, which is beyond all perception and experience. When someone talks about transmission, be on guard. Ask yourself: 'Why am I interested in this?'

Imitation: Not everyone is supposed to be a perfect guru living in a cave. On the contrary, if every human being went off to live in a cave on their own, there would be no humanity left. The play of consciousness manifests in different forms: everyone walks the path that's right for them and, after awakening, lives life in his or her own way. Imitating other people's behaviour is no guarantee of progress, and obviously bears no relation to the spontaneous behaviour shown by those who are awake.

If you have come to the end of the search, then that's that. You want to go and sit in a cave? Great. You prefer to run a real Zen monastery? Awesome. You want to grow plants? Go for it. Have a family? Okay. You prefer to keep meditating? Why not. You want to be an artist? Good for you. Are you going to be emotionally attached to any of these activities? Of course not. It is exactly through that freedom—the freedom from the fear that is inherent in the 'I-identity'—that true love and creativity can manifest.

Fake centres: The true Buddhist masters of Japan (Zen), China (Ch'an), Korea (Son), Tibet and Vietnam were very careful to maintain effective teaching methods in tandem with rigorous discipline. And this produced results, in the form of enlightenment. However, centuries of carefully guarded tradition have been thrown out of the window by, for example, the fake Zen centres which have sprung up in the Netherlands, which claim to be 'close to the market' and run aggressive programmes of expansion. There's a video you can find online in which these fake Zen 'teachers' are all singing songs together—like a big Zen party.

The money-obsessed 'master' (and we're talking millions here) who runs this organisation actively recruits new students, virtually guaranteeing that, within a couple of years, they will become Zen teachers (whatever he means by that). During this period, of course, substantial monthly payments must be made to the 'master'. He himself never actually trained for very long with a true Zen master, never received *inka* (recognition of enlightenment by a true Zen master), and so the whole edifice of his teachings is based on lies.

In fact, to elaborate on the activities of his 'I-identity', he has built his own personal website. On another website, under the label of 'Zen.nl', his business continues to expand. This website provides a clear example of all the absurdities of the spiritual swamp: Zen holidays, Zen philosophy weeks, Zen videos, Zen coaches, Zen teachers, a Zen shop. It's a prime case in point of the way an ancient take-action approach can be distorted into a hideous commercialized stay-trapped approach. Its raison d'être is to sell the impossible, to market a whole host of ways in which the 'I-identity' can supposedly find peace, energy, insight and, of course, happiness. The fact that not a single person in this movement, teacher or student, ever questions the 'I' itself is not mentioned. Clearly, so far as these students are concerned, the 'I-identity' loves the idea of becoming a Zen teacher—especially the part where they open their own business and charge people for superficial courses in mindfulness. Becoming a Zen teacher in this organisation means that any hope of true awakening has immediately gone straight down the drain.

This is just one example, but this kind of thing can be seen all over the world. Honest take-action approaches that have been carefully preserved for centuries are distorted by fake 'masters', who ensure that thousands of students are firmly stuck in the spiritual swamp, possibly for good.

If you feel that you need the guidance of a true master, stay away from any commercial organisation, from all this popular commercialized spiritual garbage, from any set-up giving undue prominence to words like 'peace', 'Zen', 'love' or 'mindfulness'. Instead, difficult though it may be in this day and age, search for a genuine Zen, Ch'an, Son, Tao or other enlightened master. Then be completely sincere, persistent and honest in your practice.

Knowing it all: Knowing is a function of the analytical mind, and thinking you know it all is totally egocentric. Always be on guard for feelings of superiority: examples of 'I-identity' inflation (ego-inflation) can be seen everywhere.

17. Esotericism

Ignorance about the 'mechanics' of the process of enlightenment in general, let alone the esoteric traditions and their related energetic practices, is widespread among western spiritual seekers and teachers. But do you, in fact, need to know about the 'energetic' mechanisms which lead to enlightenment? No. So long as you are honest and persistent in meditation or self-enquiry, the process will occur. Such knowledge will, however, enable one to avoid the pitfalls along the way.

Most esoteric practices and traditions are based on a trinity, in the sense that the 'I-identity' (also called: ego, soul, son, self, nafs, nirmanakaya, etc) can only surrender to the absolute (also called: Infinity, Brahman, Shiva, Wu chi, Allah, God/Father, Self, Buddha-nature, Dharmakaya, etc) after it has dissolved/resolved itself through universal energy (also called: Shakti, universal life-force, Holy Spirit, Sambhogakaya, etc). As a result of this process, a person becomes enlightened (also called: a Buddha, the Son of God, the Nirmanakaya, etc). Many different terms have been used in many eastern and some western esoteric traditions, but it all boils down in essence to the trinity of the 'I-identity'/Energy/Absolute. This concept of the trinity can also elucidate the physical and energetic processes that lead to enlightenment.

Ultimately speaking, there is only the absolute, which means that form/energy/absolute are all one and the same, in the same way as water/ice/vapour are all essentially the same. It is not that the absolute transcends the levels of form and energy: they are indivisible. While the concept of the trinity allows for the intellectual understanding of the absolute as it manifests on the levels of form and energy, for an enlightened being, these divisions no longer exist.

The 'I-identity' comprises identification with seven sheaths (or bodies): the physical body; the energy body (consisting of what are called meridians in Chinese medicine, through which chi flows to concentrate in dantians; alternatively, in India, we would speak of nadis, through which prana flows to concentrate in chakras); the lower mental body (worldly thoughts, emotions and desire-impulses); the higher mental body (thoughts and desire-impulses concerned with enlightenment); the astral body (containing karmic seed tendencies, which are reflected in the physical, energetic and lower/higher mental bodies); the etheric body (which is a subtle energetic reflection of the astral body); and the causal body (the final sheath, consisting of universal energy, the universal life-force, Shakti, Holy Spirit, Sambhogakaya, etc).

In connection with this causal body, it is important to state that chi (or prana) is different from universal energy. There are many different kinds of chi and other lower energies, but they all originate from the one universal energy. The causal body intersects with the physical body at the heart-centre (which in Hinduism is called the Hridayam, in Buddhism the Tathagatagarbha, and in Christianity the Sacred Heart).

And all sheaths are essentially one: the physical body is, for example, a reflection of the energy body, so if you work on the energy body, perhaps through acupuncture, the physical body is affected and can if necessary be healed.

So the 'I-identity' comprises these seven sheaths (bodies), and it is these sheaths which conceal your 'true nature' (the absolute). By means of sustained effort and intense meditation (deliberately focusing consciousness—your attention—on itself), you can let go of your 'I-identification' with these sheaths: in other words, your identification with the physical body, with the energy body, with thinking, with desires, etc, falls away.

The 'I-identity' (the root, as it were, of one's soul) functions as a 'knot' connecting the physical and the absolute. If in meditation one repeatedly traces back the 'I-identity' to its source, over and over again, all the way down to the final sheath, the causal body eventually dissolves, the 'knot' is undone and enlightenment occurs. In other words, the 'I-identity', comprising the identification (contraction) of consciousness with the first six sheaths, is dissolved when the universal energy which is the final sheath dissolves the heart-knot.

In India this union is called Shiva-Shakti; in Taoism, 'the return to the Wu Chi' or the reunion of man and Tao. Zen calls it 'the moment of realising the unity of Mind and the substance which constitutes reality', while Christianity refers to the holy communion of the Father and the Holy Spirit, leading to an enlightened Son. Buddhism talks about the union of the Sambhogakaya-Dharmakaya, and specifically in Tibetan Buddhism we have the combination of the practices of Trekcho and Togal.

This is the true experience/moment of enlightenment, when the 'I-identity' surrenders to the absolute, once and for all. After enlightenment, there is no longer 'I-identification' with a body, a mind, a heart-knot, or anything else. All 'I-identification' is resolved. Form, universal energy and the absolute are henceforth united. (Particularly in Buddhist (Zen, Ch'an, Son, Tibetan) traditions, there is a strong emphasis on the need for intense meditation after an initial awakening has occurred, to enable true surrender, and the manifestation of the absolute at the level of form and energy.) This does not mean that one ceases to exist or function as a physical body, or as any of the other bodies for that matter. These 'bodies' do not die—an enlightened being still appears in a body, can still think, can express the realisation of the absolute in his or her unique way (some Zen masters, for example, were also revered as great artists or poets). It is the 'I-identification' with these 'bodies' that disappears and that, ultimately, is replaced by the realisation of the absolute.

When a person becomes enlightened, the absolute manifests/is reflected on the level of form and energy. In the presence of an enlightened master, you can really feel the Holy Spirit of God, the Shakti of Shiva, the universal energy of the absolute. It is this 'power' which allows an enlightened person to truly live in a state of permanent surrender.

This is what differentiates the many western spiritual teachers who get stuck in the 'being' state (often charging money for their teachings) from a truly enlightened master (a true Tao, Dzogchen or Zen master, for example; or a Buddha or a Ramana Maharshi) who 'radiates'/manifests profound peace and tranquillity.

Ultimately, there is only the absolute; in reality there are no divisions, no separation. The search for enlightenment is the search for the absolute, and the trinity (which is to be found in many esoteric teachings) allows for the understanding of the absolute as it manifests on the levels of form and energy.

Relative reality is not 'unreal', a 'dream', or just

'emptiness'—it is the manifestation of the absolute on the levels of form and energy, which are in essence, of course, one and the same. Breaking your 'I-identification' with the relative reality of form and energy—'waking up to the absolute'—is the essence of the struggle for enlightenment.

In terms of the sheaths (bodies), the trap of the 'being' state—often mistaken for enlightenment and the trap into which nowadays most students and spiritual teachers fall, particularly in the west—can be explained as follows: the 'being' state arises when the 'I-identification' with the lower and higher mental bodies is broken. As a result, identification with thoughts falls away, the mind goes blank, and it appears that there is no longer identification with anything at all. The result is an empty mind, less identification with the physical body, a stronger energy body (because more energy is now available), an increased sense of joy and a sense of oneness with everything.

However, tracing back the source of the 'I-identity' simply to the lower and higher mental bodies (in short, to thinking) and letting go of that identification is by no means the end of seeking. One must trace back the source of the 'I-identity' through *all* the sheaths.

Let me repeat that knowledge of the 'energetic' process of enlightenment is not a prerequisite—the prerequisites for enlightenment are simply honesty and persistence. What has been provided in the preceding paragraphs is a brief summary of the essence of many esoteric/spiritual traditions.

Moreover, it is not intended that all these words should explain the absolute, since an explanation of the absolute is clearly impossible. This chapter is simply intended to provide a conceptual context for the self-enquiry process: from total identification with an 'I-identity' all the way through to surrender to the absolute.

I have no wish to complicate matters by going into further detail—not because I am unaware of the finer points of the esoteric traditions but because, in the end, conceptual knowledge is unimportant, despite the numerous books and entire encyclopaedias that exist in all the major spiritual traditions. It is also very important to remember that spiritual/esoteric traditions have been arguing with each other about conceptual interpretations for centuries, completing missing the point. The point, after all, is to make the effort—not to get lost in words.

Many words and many different terms are used in this book, but they all point in the same direction: they are all aimed at demonstrating the way many spiritual traditions have an essential 'take-action' approach at their core. The spiritual swamp is so vast nowadays that it is very difficult to find effective directions leading out of it. This book, while honouring the energetic/esoteric depth of true spiritual traditions, keeps things as simple as possible, and never ignores the fact that serious study and intensive practice and effort are necessary to begin the process of detachment from the 'I-identity'. And once you set out to truly break away from your 'I-identity', you will find that you naturally start seeking out the information you need.

Whilst, during the last century, Tibetan and other forms of Buddhism have become better known, and an increasing amount of attention has been paid to Indian Yoga, Christian Mysticism/Hermeticism and Kashmir Shaivism, one central eastern tradition which has remained shrouded in mystery is Taoism.

Taoism, which goes back almost ten thousand years, is an advanced esoteric system of energy cultivation and spiritual development which can only be understood through dedicated practice. Anyone studying eastern spiritual traditions in depth will come to realise that most have their roots in Taoism, or have at some point 'branched off' from Taoism.

Some authors mention Chuang-Tzu, while others may quote from the *Tao Te Ch'ing* or similar ancient texts but, generally speaking, most stop there. Accurate translations of ancient Taoist texts are hard to find, and it's harder still to really understand such texts, as the Taoist masters passed on their knowledge verbally, or cloaked the meaning behind their techniques in synonyms and metaphors. A few Taoist masters have revealed a few secrets, but the understanding of the secret energetic esoteric techniques used by Taoists has only really become clear in the west since Mantak Chia made them public.

Taoism—the genuine kind of Taoism—is a take-action approach. Why? Because it stresses the necessity for extensive practice and introspection, in solitude. This is not the commercialised version of Taoism, nor the kind where you spend your life in a Taoist group or become part of a Taoist organisation, but the kind of Taoism where a true master shares his teachings with an adept, who then goes off to practise. This kind of genuine master/disciple relationship can also be found in, for example, Tibetan Buddhism, Zen and in other traditions, but it is becoming increasingly rare.

According to Taoist masters, at the highest level of Taoist alchemy, 'an awakening to that which is eternal and enduring occurs'—in other words, a surrender to the absolute. However, if you ever study the Taoist system, you might find some of the terms confusing. In Taoism, in brief, the *ching* (sexual energy) is transformed into chi (bodily energy), which is transformed into *shen* (spirit), followed by a return to the *wu chi* (the absolute).

In Taoist practices (and also in some Yoga or Tibetan Buddhist practices), the tremendous energy released through the conservation and recycling of sexual energy (ching) is used to dissolve all dualistic boundaries between body, mind and the universe; the result is surrender to the absolute.

A Taoist thoroughly prepares the body for the final influx of universal energy by first thoroughly opening the meridians. Such traditions do not struggle with the mind, but rather promote practices which gradually increase the energy level to a point where it can be utilised to dissolve the dualistic energy patterns (boundaries) of mind and body. (As stated in chapter 7, the Taoist techniques for recycling sexual energy are very useful for someone who is contemplating serious self-enquiry. Ignoring or blocking sexual energy will never work. Either you transcend it—which for most people takes a lot of discipline and effort in meditation—or you transform it by using, for example, Taoist techniques. For further information, see Mantak Chia's *Taoist Secrets of Love, Healing Love through the Tao, The Multi-orgasmic Couple*, etc.)

So yes, the principle goal of Taoist alchemy is also enlightenment, but some masters go on to refine their bodily energy—with extraordinary results, known in Taoism as the levels of immortality.

Immortality here does not mean the immortality of the 'I-identity', the idea that the 'I' will live forever. The 'I-identity' is limited, mortal: the absolute is unlimited; and, in a manner of speaking, the total transcendence of all identification with a limited 'I-identity' could be described as 'immortality'. However, this is not what Taoists mean.

What is meant by immortality in Taoism is not only the attainment of enlightenment and the transcendence of the identification with a limited 'I-identity', but the continual refinement of bodily energy until it also totally dissolves into the absolute.

Now that Mantak Chia has brought the Taoist energy practices to the west, an in-depth study and practice of Taoism can clearly explain: the ascension and resurrection of Jesus and other masters; the rainbow body (or immortal spirit body, when the bodies of Taoist, Yogi and Tibetan masters dissolve at death; also called Soruba Samadhi in India or jalus in Tibet); the spirit/immortal body; breatharianism (masters living without food) and other such 'supernatural' events. (For further details, look into the universal healing system of Taoism, especially the higher practices: fusion, lesser kan and li, greater kan and li, greatest kan and li, sealing of the five senses, reunion of man and heaven, reunion of man and Tao.)

Similar advanced energetic practices can also be found in Tibetan Dzogchen Buddhism, Bon, Tantric Buddhism (Vajrayana) and forms of tantric Yoga. Dzogchen and Taoism even distinguish three levels of the rainbow body: partly dissolving at death, totally dissolving at death, dissolving while still alive. Dzogchen claims to be the highest and purest form of Buddhism, because so many masters throughout history, after receiving proper instruction, attained the rainbow body. Whilst this claim is probably a little extreme, it is unlikely to be a coincidence that Taoism and Dzogchen, both spiritual traditions with roots stretching back many thousands of years, each clearly state that attainment of the rainbow body is possible, and that many masters have been able to dissolve their physical body into the absolute. In this context, the resemblance to the story of the ascension and resurrection of Jesus is striking. And since the physical body (form) and energy are in essence part of the absolute, it seems logical that a transformation (return) from one to the other should be possible.

So yes, it seems that the practice—after enlightenment—of dissolving the physical body into the absolute is a possibility. However, proper instruction from a master is essential.

If you think this is all bullshit, fine. Be very sceptical—as I was myself. Start investigating for yourself, perhaps by studying Taoism or Dzogchen. Whilst information on the highest levels of esoteric Taoism is now available, however, much of the Dzogchen teachings have not yet been translated into English, and so, to learn about Dzogchen's advanced energetic practices, one would have to learn Tibetan and get proper instruction from a true master. Needless to say, for that reason, my own knowledge of the subject is severely limited.

Once you have experienced the reality of chi, once you have torn down some of the boundaries of the 'I-identity', the realisation will dawn that many things you thought were impossible are actually possible.

Be on guard, however, because, in the beginning, it is easy to get lost in energetic, occult or spiritual experiences and lose focus. Nowadays, most practitioners of Taoism and other esoteric traditions, especially in the west, just toy with energy practices at a superficial level, and never surrender to the absolute. They never come to realise that energetic and spiritual experiences, however seductive, must be discarded on the path towards the discovery of what the 'I' really is.

The point of awakening is not to obtain control over

the physical, energetic and spiritual realms, nor to acquire special powers such as extraordinary longevity, telepathy or clairvoyance, however tempting such distractions might seem. Nor is it in the least important what other people have done or achieved: this can only be a distraction from the enquiry into the reality of the 'I'. The central point is to find out who it is who is experiencing in the first place, without losing focus, getting lost in the spiritual swamp or in esoteric studies, or falling into the trap of the 'being' state.

So why even mention esotericism in the first place? Well, I guess knowing about the sheaths and the process of detachment from them, for example, can help explain why the 'being' state is so often mistaken for enlightenment, and hence save you time in the spiritual swamp. And at the beginning of a true struggle with the 'I-identity', it is useful to have some knowledge of chi or energetic experiences, so that you can keep pushing forward when the 'I-identity' tries to hide in the false sense of energetic serenity.

In essence, however, no matter what version of the take-action approach one might take, it all comes down to the same thing: being honest, focused and alone.

Why say or write anything at all, if the absolute cannot be known or experienced? Well, if nobody had talked or written in the past about the take-action approach to genuine self-enquiry, how would we even know that enlightenment was possible? To insist that nobody should talk or write directly about awakening is often an excuse used by ineffective teachers who are proponents of the stay-trapped approach, to cover up their own lack of focus and clarity on the subject.

Let's clarify with an example. Think of the largest canyon you can imagine (the Grand Canyon, say). On one side it's always raining—this represents the prison of the 'I-identity'; and on the other side it's always sunny—this represents the 'being' state. A charlatan on the sunny side describes to the people on the rainy side how amazing life is on the sunny side: 'There's so much light here! There's silence, awareness, peace, oneness, unity, bliss, presence... If you can just be aware, it will stop raining. There is, in fact, nobody perceiving the rain.'

On the rainy side, nevertheless, it keeps on raining. How is his advice ever going to help the people there? How can they get to the other side? And the people on the rainy side actually pay to hear him say these things!

A true master/awakened being tells the people on the rainy side to look for a rope, to climb down to the bottom of the canyon, to cross a river full of crocodiles and to crawl back up again. He doesn't hide the fact that the journey (which represents the long struggle with the 'I'-identity) is an incredibly dangerous one. And the advice he gives is free, although it is rarely well received by the people on the rainy side—some may go so far as to crucify him one day, just because of what he says. Most of the people on the rainy side simply don't want to hear the advice of the master: they prefer to keep listening to—and paying—the charlatan. They prefer to stand in the rain forever, because it's familiar, and so much easier than climbing down: fear is a powerful deterrent.

Nevertheless, there may be one sincere person in the group who realises that the true master could be right, who finds a rope, climbs down, swims through the crocodiles and climbs back up again to the other side. Finally, after this journey, standing on the sunny side, he says: 'Amazing—it's paradise—it's all, and it's nothing!'

He doesn't realise that he's trapped himself again (in the 'being' state—'the pit of formlessness') but, luckily for him, the master comes along and tells him that the sunny side is also just an illusion, that he has not yet finished, that he still has a long way to go.

So now that the difference between the stay-trapped approach and the take-action approach is clear, the obvious question left for us is, 'So how do I begin?'

18. Begin

There are innumerable ways in which the 'I-identity' keeps itself trapped, and the result is a society in which people try to be 'someone' in innumerable different ways. Human history, in short, comes down to the repetition of the same pattern—over and over and over again: people trying to be someone, so that the 'I-identity' can stay alive.

In the beginning, you may notice that people around you will discourage you in every way they can from embarking on a path of true self-enquiry, because this goes against the grain of what society's all about. A flock of sheep does not like to see any of its members leave. So if you decide to leave the flock, do not stay on the horizon where the flock can see you and where you can see the flock, because it will make leaving a lot harder.

During my own struggles, my attempts to have 'a foot in both camps' would not only end up almost ripping me apart in conflict and frustration, but also caused quite a lot of unnecessary suffering for friends and family. Often, I was a pain in the ass to be around. Good friends were abandoned, relationships were destroyed and the best friendship of all, with Michael, also had to go out of the window when I realised that the 'being' state was not the end.

This is all part of the price you have to pay. Since in essence everybody is suffering, the fact that you might temporarily have to increase the suffering of others by moving away from them is not a reason to stay with them. If you are not willing to do that, you might as well give up immediately.

In order to break away from your 'I-identity' without causing too much unnecessary suffering to others, it is essential to break away from society and everyone you know as swiftly as possible. This process will always be messy, and there is virtually no avoiding it... But the minimizing of 'collateral damage' is recommended, and the only part of my path I would change—if I could—would be the suffering I caused to others.

Even so, would I do it again? Yes, definitely: there was in any case no other option. And was it worth it? This has nothing to do with 'worth'—there is simply no other way forward.

Moreover, in order to make real progress, you need to do exactly the opposite of the usual practice in psychological and spiritual circles: read books and articles that are *not* well-known or fashionable, seek out the reading material that is hard to find, that which is rarely read at all. Then discard all the books, and do what nobody really wants to do: be alone.

'But I want to help the world,' you may argue. 'I want to do good as well as making spiritual progress.'

Before trying to help the world, a true student of life first needs to address the question, who is the one who wants to help the world? Who is observing the world in the first place? If the answer is 'me', ask yourself: 'What *is* me?' A true student always starts with the basics: 'Who am I?', 'What exactly is the "me"?', 'What is this "world"?' Before seeking to help 'the world', ask yourself, 'Am I still emotionally attached to the idea and the feeling of being a separate "I-identity"?' Because if you are, there is work to be done. Taking action to help the world, whilst at the same time having no idea of who the one is who is taking the actions, basically means allowing the 'I-identity' out on a blind rampage. However good the intentions, this will inevitably end in frustration and suffering.

Some people might take the view: 'If you don't help the world, if you don't care about anything anymore, you're being extremely selfish.' On the contrary: by observing that belief in the 'I-identity' is the fundamental distortion, the one which turns the world into a hostile place where one can never be at peace, one can finally start on the struggle through which, eventually, one moves beyond all the distortions and misperceptions lying at the heart of selfish and neurotic behaviour. To embark on that struggle I call the taking of true responsibility. And only through the dissolution of the illusion of separation can real compassion arise.

Look, for example, at an animal or plant and ask yourself, 'Why don't animals and plants worry?' The simple answer is: because they don't think. Have you ever seen an obese fish, a suicidal dog, an aggressive flower, a neurotic bird, a drug-addicted tree, a schizophrenic cat, a depressed plant? No, of course not, except where animals have been put in zoos or imprisoned in huge industrial farms, or are kept as pets living in unnatural circumstances and fed totally unnatural food. Human beings are the ones who display all kinds of insane behaviour, and still we think we are superior to animals and plants. And it is exactly because of all that thinking that our behaviour is so totally insane.

So the question arises: 'Why *do* I think?' And then: 'Who is it that is thinking?'

Some reckon that the natural human state is one of ignorance and savagery, but this is a claim made by 'people' (those trapped in the 'I-identity') in relation to other 'people' (also trapped in the 'I-identity'). Ignorance, resistance, fear, imbalance, savagery and all other forms of madness are quite normal in the realm of the 'I-identity'. Similarly, good/bad, wrong/right, worse/better are part and parcel of the dualistic universe which the 'I-identity' perceives. After the collapse of the 'I-identity', none of this applies.

◎ ◎ ◎

The spiritual swamp is full of techniques based in the stay-trapped approach, and over the years countless vague and confusing books and teachers have been filling up the spiritual swamp. Every year, the swamp of confusion spreads as vast quantities of new material advocating this approach are published online or in print. The fake teachers promoting the stay-trapped approach are 'somewhere', in some state, and attach importance to the fact that others should awaken. To the enlightened, there are no others, since there is no separation between the illusory 'I-identity' and 'others'.

Let's emphasize again that there is nothing wrong with teaching people about meditation, mindfulness and other techniques so they can feel better and more at ease. Commercializing it and selling it as enlightenment is not so fantastic.

Before even considering embarking on genuine self-enquiry, it is important to understand what the process of enlightenment really entails; and the ability to discriminate between books or teachings that advocate a stay-trapped approach from those that sincerely and accurately promote the take-action approach is critical.

And why do most books or teachings keep you trapped? Because books that state that true self-enquiry requires strenuous effort just do not sell. The 'I-identity' prefers to read about effortlessness and love. It does not want to read about its own demise, to contemplate being alone, exerting real effort for years on end. Most books simply encourage you to wallow in mental inertia.

So what kind of books might be useful in the beginning? Those that really challenge you, that make you question everything, that make you doubt everything you ever thought was true, that encourage a sincere and focused take-action approach.

During my own search, and also for the purposes of writing this book, I did a lot of research into spiritual, philosophical and esoteric traditions. What I found was that nowadays the spiritual swamp is vast: so many different systems which simply feed the 'I-identity', thousands of different teachers, millions of energy healers, an infinite number of self-help and healing modalities.

And even if one were to become an expert in these traditions, one would not come a single step closer to even beginning the true struggle to find out what the 'I' really is. It is easy enough to earn a PhD in religion, to be a philosopher and toy with words, to become an expert in esoteric traditions—it is far from easy to be alone.

In the final analysis, the number of books which I actually found useful at the beginning of my own struggles could be counted on the fingers of two hands. I have intentionally made reference to only a few books here, as these are the ones which you may well find useful yourself if you truly struggle with the 'I-identity'. I don't like to recommend particularly esoteric books to those who are just embarking on the struggle, especially since spiritual practice starts with emptying the mind of concepts, not filling it up.

Once your search is underway, your own curiosity will naturally lead you to seek out more books. And when things get really serious and you begin to shed the layers of your 'I-identity', you may become interested in the kind of esoteric material which will help explain what is actually happening. (For clear information on esoteric subjects, for example, look at the work of L Ron Gardner, especially the recommended esoteric bibliographies at the end of his books.)

But in the beginning, it is, indeed, useful to read a few particularly focused books that encourage an honest take-action approach. To name a few examples:

- *Mud and water*, a collection of talks by the Zen Master Bassui

- *The Albigen Papers* by Richard Rose

- *I am That* by Sri Nisargadatta Maharaj

- *Spiritual enlightenment: the damnedest thing* by Jed McKenna

- *Skeletons* by Ikkyu

- *The Zen teaching of Huang Po* translated by John Blofeld

Further recommendations are given at the end of this book, and if you want to read still more, look at the recommended reading sections within these books.

The material you'll find in these works is focused indeed. Take, for example, these lines from Bassui:

'If you simply try to stop the movement of consciousness and consider this enlightenment, this will put an iron wall between you and enlightenment. You must look at the self like one with fresh hatred viewing an enemy; only then will

you succeed.'

'How incredible! Today's students of the Way are of inferior character, and their aspiration is superficial. They give no thought to the truth of the great matter of life and death. Though they go to teachers everywhere, they don't want to penetrate completely, all the way to the bottom.'

'Turning inward, turning outwards, destroying everything completely, you will for the first time begin to achieve the proper results.'

Of course, after a while every book becomes another mental obstacle, and one has to discard all books and all attachment to them once and for all. In the end, what matters is the struggle, the honesty, the determination—and, so far as that's concerned, books are ultimately useless.

Whilst this book gives a brief summary of the essence of most spiritual traditions, obviously it can never cover them all in every detail, and that is not its point. It simply describes some aspects of the mental, economic and spiritual swamp, some of the hurdles one might need to jump, providing in addition tips on how to focus and 'set course' out of the swamp.

This book was not written with the aim simply of telling a good story, nor to bolster the 'I-identity' of the one who writes. For some reason I was lucky enough to suffer and struggle intensely at a young age, while still managing to maintain some focus. I consider this suffering as the greatest gift because, without it, I'd probably have ended up as a miserable banker in some office somewhere.

You might be wondering, 'Who does he think he is, saying all this? Why did he write this book in the first place?'

Well, I simply got fed up of being enslaved by a mind I didn't understand, an 'I-identity' made up of ignorance, pretence and suffering. The ensuing struggle to figure out what the 'I' really is (or, more precisely, what it is not) went on for years. At last the 'being' state arose, the most convincing trick the 'I-identity' can pull on anyone struggling with this search—and when it became clear that the 'being' state was not in fact the end, the struggle continued.

It is becoming harder and harder to encounter teachers and teachings who are aware of the many traps of the 'I-identity'. And so the main reason for writing this book is to elucidate that final trap, to explain the difference between the 'being' state and enlightenment.

Masters and also laymen throughout human history have surrendered to the absolute and, although rare, there are obviously real teachers and teachings still available that promote an honest take-action approach, without charge. Those who have attempted to navigate the spiritual swamp will feel profound gratitude and respect for such teachers.

So if the 'I-identity' has collapsed, who has written all this? An 'I'—which is a term that describes something that both is and is not—is a paradox, agreed. That kind of expression is part of the stay-trapped approach. To actually figure out who has written this—and who is reading this—the only way forward is genuine self-enquiry, because only by breaking down the 'I-identity' will the paradox resolve.

The process of self-enquiry begins when you close your eyes, see the thoughts streaming past and ask yourself: 'Who is it who is seeing all these thoughts? Who is feeling this energy?' The answer 'me' or 'I am' will immediately arise in the mind. So next, ask yourself: 'And who is observing the "me" or the "I am"?'

Anything that arises in the mind is obviously not who you really are, because there is still 'something' observing. As stated earlier, we can never be one hundred percent certain that any subjective experience is really true, which is why the struggle for enlightenment is the search for an absolute truth—the absolute. The 'I-identity' keeps itself alive by believing that its perceptions are absolutely real, by identifying with them; and it is by dis-identifying from them, by breaking the emotional attachment to them, that the 'I-identity' begins to crumble. If I can see my name, I cannot be my name. If I can see my thoughts, I cannot be my thoughts. If I can see the thought 'I', I cannot be the thought 'I'. If I can feel energy, I cannot be energy. And so forth, and so forth.

The 'I-identity', however, will fight back: 'you' most certainly do not want to become 'non-you'. The 'I-identity' manifests in innumerable ways: identification with name, body, family, country, nationality, friends, a 'digital identity', hobbies, ideas, convictions, religion, etc. It will look for con-firmation of its existence, pursuing any belief or emotional attachment it can find (to people, groups, ideas, concepts, feelings, trains of thought, etc) in order to derail the process of dis-identification.

Emotional attachments originate in fear, and fear is in essence a thought (and feeling) that you are not going to be able to have whatever it is you think you need—for example, your body, your money, a future, your 'I-identity', etc. If you say to someone, 'Imagine not owning a house or a car... imagine having no job', you can see the fear in their face, the fear of not having material possessions and social status, the fear of not being 'someone'. When someone is dying or confronted with death, that is when they are most scared: because they are scared that they will lose their 'I'.

Nobody likes to have their 'reality' disrupted, and when the 'I-identity' starts to wobble, extreme fear will arise. There is no greater enemy than one's own fears, and it is by confronting these fears, in solitude, that true self-enquiry begins. A genuine process of awakening will lead to increasing amounts of inner doubt as well, especially in the beginning. That inner doubt, in combination with effort and focus, will be the fuel that powers your self-enquiry. Nisargadatta Maharaj is very clear about the fact that you have to become totally obsessed to find out who you really are—otherwise your enquiry will be fruitless.

The removal of the mental boundaries which the emotional attachments create can be done effectively by focusing consciousness (your attention) on itself. In the beginning, this meditative practice will dissolve emotional attachments, habit-energies, defilements, desire-impulses, etc. These are all deeply ingrained, so this is tough work, especially because the ability to concentrate is still weak at this stage, while ignorance and pointless mental activity are widespread.

After a while, the main practice becomes the constant focusing of consciousness on itself, while tracing the 'I-identity' back to its source. If, for example, you are thinking, ask yourself: 'Who is thinking?' If you feel amazing energy, ask yourself: 'Who is feeling this energy?' If you think you know who you are, ask yourself: 'Who am I?'

The next step is the ability to abide for longer periods of time in a profound state of surrender (esoterically, this means you connect with the causal body/universal energy/holy spirit, etc, as explained in chapter 17). As long as you continue to identify with the mind and/or body, the heart-knot will not be dissolved, so persistence here is crucial. Ultimately, one abides in and functions from a state of surrender all the time.

So this whole process is a slow and agonising one, to say the least. This is the kind of thing that happens in the hour upon hour, year upon year of meditation practised in a real Zen monastery, for example. This is why real Advaita masters encourage you to focus constantly on the feeling 'I am' while discarding all other perceptions, until the 'I-identity' finally yields.

It is important to state as well that real meditation is not just about 'letting go' or 'emptying yourself'. Simply 'letting go' will not get you anywhere: 'letting go' has to be combined with focus. So meditation is a combination of focus and 'letting go', of being conscious (alertness) and surrendering (calmness) at the same time. The focus aims at trying to find out what the 'I-identity' really is (self-enquiry). The 'letting go' is the surrender of all that the 'I-identity' is not—which, in the end, amounts to everything. Take-action approaches combine these two aspects of meditation into a truly effective tool.

Another effective practice is to try to write down who it is that you think you are, in the knowledge that anything you may write is essentially *not* who you really are. In this way, with the intention of finding out who you really are—or, more precisely, what you are not, you can work your way through the thoughts, feelings, emotions and concepts which form the structure of your 'I-identity'. However, to break through the 'being' state, to let go of the final 'I-identification' and dissolve the heart-knot, long hard effort in meditation is usually also necessary.

These practices—meditation on its own, or writing in

conjunction with meditation—are both effective, and both require solitude, total dedication, honesty and persistence. So any talk you might hear about people 'developing themselves spiritually' whilst still in a regular job or whilst maintaining relationships is obviously indicative of a stay-trapped approach. Both methods will take time—a considerable amount of time. Once the process has begun, however, do not stop until you are done: any attempt to be both in the normal everyday world and free of it will lead to extreme frustration for you and for everyone around you.

After a while, you will come to realize that the point of all this effort is not actually to find 'an answer', because any 'answer' can be observed and will thus subsequently be discarded. The point is to take apart the 'I-identity', the one who is asking the questions in the first place. As stated earlier, the process of awakening is the step by step dis-identification from all subjective experiences—physical, mental, energetic, spiritual, including dis-identification from both the 'I-identity' and from the 'being' state. It is literally to break out of an illusion: the illusion that you are a separate 'I-identity', the illusion that reality is absolutely real, and the illusion that any subjective experiences are absolutely true.

All mental, conceptual and intellectual activity which fosters dualism has to be discarded. This includes, for example, the idea that enlightenment can be achieved or grasped; the idea that there is a difference between enlightened and unenlightened; the need to differentiate between reality and illusion. Many people stay trapped in the spiritual swamp for decades or even a lifetime because of their unwillingness to surrender the idea that the 'I' can achieve enlightenment. This idea is the biggest boost the 'I-identity' can receive: it's what is guaranteed to keep the mind going indefinitely, just like a cat chasing its tail, because it is the one thing it can never achieve.

When there is no longer identification with a 'questioner', there are no more questions, hence no answers are needed. When the necessary colossal effort has been made to deconstruct the 'I-identity', one day it will collapse—partially—and the 'being' state will arise. And as I have already said, while the 'being' state may seem like the final liberation, there is still further to go.

Although everything may now seem perfect, try to become aware of the very subtle 'I-identification' which is experiencing the 'being' state. Who is it who is feeling this sense of 'being'? Who is recognising the void? Who is recognising everything in nothing? Focus, be sincere and, instead of returning to society now to share your revelation by teaching others and talking to spiritual groups, do the exact opposite: remain alone, for even longer. And keep on tracing the 'I' back to its source.

19. There is only one koan

Zen koans are paradoxical riddles which Zen masters give their students to enable them to break down the attachment to the mind. The Zen Master Ikkyu wrote the following about koans:

'There is only one koan—"you".'

Nothing can ever be wrong, but if things appear to be wrong and you want to do something about it, pursue that feeling that there must be more to life than living as a slave to your 'I-identity'.

Everything in 'your' life will disappear: your 'I-identity', your life, your family, your friends, your possessions, this solar system, this universe... Everything. Nothing was ever 'yours' in the first place. Even though it can never be experienced, the absolute is the only unlimited truth there is. Purpose is illusory, a fabrication of the mind, but if I had to name one purpose in life, it would be surrender to the absolute.

Thoughts, beer, consciousness, positive interest, the heart-knot, food, questions, sex, forest gardens, chi, truth, Taoist energy techniques for men and women, esotericism, aids-babies, the 'being' state, money, the take-action approach versus the stay-trapped approach, enlightenment . . . Some crucial subjects—some or all of which you may at some point come across—have been discussed.

Thinking you know who you are means being in prison. Ultimately, the only thing that matters is figuring out what that 'I' is—un-knowing what you think you know for sure. And whilst doing so, beware of the many stay-trapped approaches that are prevalent in the spiritual swamp; beware of the trap of the 'being' state, and of teachers who ask for money or donations.

This book is written in direct and unequivocal language. Why? People have extreme difficulty in challenging their fixed ideas, opinions, beliefs and assumptions, especially when they confront the 'I-identity'; the fear that arises is so powerful. The only way to get rid of it is to stand your ground and face it. Fail to destroy boundaries and suffering will go on. In the end you will lie on your deathbed in deep fear, trapped in the illusory thought, 'Oh my god... I am going to die'.

Of course, anything in duality—including the words in this book—is contradictory. The moment a word is spoken or written, the contradictions begin. Sure, agreed: that's the nature of duality. Many words have been used in this book, but the process described can never actually be understood through words alone.

So as you hold this book, can you observe yourself holding this book?

As you read it, can you observe yourself reading?

By the way, as I have already mentioned, the moment you start really thinking about all this, life as you know it will be thrown into total disarray. The process of taking the 'I-identity' apart will become ever more extreme, because in essence you are literally taking yourself apart, taking apart all your beliefs and your sense of being a separate 'being'. So yes, this is basically the toughest ride anyone can embark upon. And anyone claiming this is an easy process, that effortlessness is the key, is promoting a stay-trapped approach.

So why would anyone do all this in the first place? Ignorance—the prison of the 'I-identity'—is not bliss. Ignorance is, in fact, hell. The enlightened state, on the other hand, is one of true liberation, acceptance, clarity, tranquillity, profound peace, fearlessness, sensitivity, humility and, of course, love. A living example that nothing is wrong, nor will it be, nor has it ever been. The fact that enlightenment is available to every human being should never be forgotten.

It is not the 'I-identity' that must find its origin, not resting content with the 'being' state—it is consciousness itself, of which the 'I' and the 'being' state are only a small part.

Thanks to today's consumer society, many spiritual teachings and teachers have been reduced to intellectualism (conceptual understanding) with a concomitant ignorance of the energetic/esoteric essentials. Nevertheless, the true requirements of the spiritual path remain the same as they have for centuries: ardent effort in meditation and/or persistent self-enquiry. Once you begin to realise what this actually means, you understand through direct experience that all words, all concepts—everything that has been said in this book—mean nothing and have nothing to do with the absolute. So you can burn this book or give it away once you've read it, as the hard part is not reading, it's actually putting in the effort.

In a moment, when you've finished the book, just put it down, go for a walk, sit down somewhere and ask yourself: 'Where has all the living I've done up to now got me? Why am I not at peace? Why am I always looking for something else? Why am I still stuck in the same mental patterns? Why am I living this life with my eyes closed?'

If you are fed up with living in the prison of the 'I-identity'—fed up with being a slave to the mental, economic and cultural patterns which totally dominate your sense of self, start struggling with your 'I'. A radical change and a confrontation with your deepest fears is the only way forward. Only then will you come to know how powerful and how deceptive the 'I-identity' really is.

Focus on the fear of being 'nobody', the need to be 'someone'.

What is looking at that thought 'I'?

Epilogue

Honesty

Focus

Alone

Recommended reading

Meditations—Marcus Aurelius

Mud and water—A collection of talks by the Zen Master Bassui

The Zen teaching of Huang Po: on the transmission of mind—translated by John Blofeld

Awakening healing energy through the Tao—Mantak Chia

Creating a forest garden—Martin Crawford

Sacred economics—Charles Eisenstein

The one straw revolution—Masanobu Fukuoka

Electrical Christianity—L Ron Gardner

Skeletons—Ikkyu

Sri Ramana Gita—Bhagavan Sri Ramana Maharshi

Spiritual enlightenment: the damnedest thing—Jed McKenna

I am That—Sri Nisargadatta Maharaj

The Albigen Papers—Richard Rose

Between I butterfly—Dirk Herre van der Veek

On the taboo against knowing who you are—Alan Watts

16707642R00079

Printed in Poland
by Amazon Fulfillment
Poland Sp. z o.o., Wrocław